THE NATCHEZ DISTRICT
AND THE AMERICAN REVOLUTION

The Natchez District and the American Revolution

by

ROBERT V. HAYNES

UNIVERSITY PRESS OF MISSISSIPPI
JACKSON

Contents

Preface

THIS study grew out of an invitation from Dr. John E. Gonzales, editor of the *Journal of Mississippi History*, to write an article on the James Willing raid for a special bicentennial issue of the *Journal*. This invitation was followed by two others. Mrs. R. A. McLemore, president-elect of the Mississippi Historical Society, asked me to give the dinner address at the association's March, 1974, meeting in Biloxi. The warm reception which I received on that occasion encouraged me to continue my research and to broaden my focus. Several months later one of my former students, Dr. Riley Venza of Murray State University, invited me to deliver a lecture on the American Revolution in the Southwest. As a result of my preparations for these speeches, I became increasingly aware of an important and largely neglected aspect of the Revolution. I also discovered that other historians were equally uninformed about the course of the Revolution in the Southwest.

Wherever I went in search of sources, librarians and archivists were there to assist me. The staff of the Mississippi Department of Archives and History went out of its way to aid me. Carl Ray, Laura D. Harrell Sturdivant, and Ronald Tomlin were always on hand when I needed them. Howard Peckham and John C. Dann of the W. L. Clements Library made my all-too-brief stay in Ann Arbor a memorable one. The staffs at the Historical Society of Pennsylvania, the State Historical Society of Wisconsin, the Library of Congress, and the National Archives were most accommodating and extremely helpful. The interlibrary loan staff at the M. D. Anderson Library of the University of Houston was helpful in locating and obtaining pertinent material from other libraries. Marian Orgain, curator of special collections at the University of Houston, assisted me in numerous ways, and Mrs. Ralph Johnston donated to the University of Houston library a valuable document which proved extremely useful to my study. Two research grants from the Office of Research at the University of Houston made it possible for me to visit distant libraries. My wife, Martha Farr Haynes, as always, served me well as typist and critic. Doug Inglis and Byrle Kynerd read the manuscript and proved to be valuable critics, although I alone am responsible for whatever errors remain.

ROBERT V. HAYNES

THE NATCHEZ DISTRICT
AND THE AMERICAN REVOLUTION

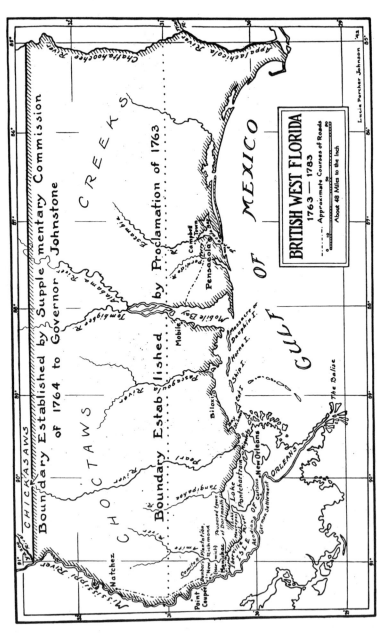

Johnson, Cecil. *British West Florida 1763–1783.* New Haven: Yale, 1943.

1

A British Possession

In 1775, when fighting broke out at Lexington and Concord between British regulars and the colonial militia of Massachusetts, Natchez was a small isolated settlement of several hundred European inhabitants located along the eastern bank of the Mississippi River approximately 240 miles north of New Orleans. Despite the prevalence of fertile lands around the little community, Natchez was only beginning to realize its long recognized potential.

The French were the first Europeans to occupy the area around what was later known as the Natchez District. As early as 1714, they had established a small trading post at Natchez landing below the steep bluff which overlooked the broad and swift-flowing Mississippi River. Although the French traders were pleased when their government erected Fort Rosalie there in 1716, later settlers who took up more permanent residence were unable to dispel the deeply ingrained suspicions of the Natchez Indians. In 1729, the Natchez unexpectedly fell upon the exposed settlement of more than 700 white and black inhabitants. Only a few settlers managed to escape the holocaust which followed. At least 229 people perished in the massacre and nearly 450 others were sold to the British or enslaved by the Natchez themselves. Although French officials in Louisiana continued to maintain a small garrison at Fort Rosalie, which they rebuilt in 1734, the Natchez District never recovered from the devastation as long as it remained a possession of France.[1]

In the 1763 Treaty of Paris which ended the Seven Years' War, Spain ceded to England all her possessions east of the Mississippi River except the Isle de Orleans, which she had obtained from France with the rest of Louisiana the year before as compensation for losing Florida. In October of 1763, the British government, as part of a general reassessment of its western policy in North America, established three new continental colonies out of the territory recently acquired from France and Spain. Two of these new provinces were located in what had previously been part of French Louisiana and Spanish Florida. While retaining the Spanish name of Florida, England, for sound administrative reasons, split the territory into two provinces. That portion east of the Apalachicola and Chattahoochee rivers was designated East Florida while the other part was named West Florida. As eventually defined in 1764, the boundaries of West Florida consisted of the Apalachicola and Chattahoochee rivers on the east, the Mississippi River on the west, the Gulf of Mexico, Lakes Pontchartrain and Maurepas, and the Iberville River on the south, and a line drawn due east from the mouth of the "Yazous" River on the north.[2]

Although not as large in size or in population as East Florida, the western province presented England with greater problems of administration. In contrast to East Florida, where European inhabitants were confined primarily to the Atlantic coast, the population of West Florida was more scattered. In 1763, when the British first took possession of the territory, a majority of the settlers resided in one of two weakly fortified coastal towns—Mobile and Pensacola. Although Pensacola was on the colony's southeastern extremity, the British placed the provincial capital there rather than in Mobile for two principal reasons. Pensacola was considered a healthier location, and its harbor was easier to defend and more suitable for commerce than Mobile's. According to Thomas Hutchins, a talented military officer and engineer who served for several years in West Florida, ocean-going vessels could not come within seven miles of Mobile. As a result, Pensacola quickly became the administrative as well as the commercial center of West Florida.[3]

At first, British officials in West Florida were unenthusiastic about the two settlements. Lieutenant Colonel Augustine Prevost, commanding officer of the Sixtieth Regiment who took possession of Pensacola from the Spaniards on August 6, 1763, and who later served as governor of East Florida, was extremely disappointed when he surveyed the town for the first time. "Pensacola is a small Village of about one hundred huts," he reported. Prevost lamented that the countryside, "from the Insuperable laziness of the Spaniards," was "still uncultivated," although the colonel was pleased to discover a few small gardens in the adjacent woods. Major William Forbes, who arrived with the Thirty-fifth Regiment on November 30, was equally unhappy with what he found. The deplorable condition of the fortifications disturbed him most. "The fort," he noted, "consists of about half a Mile of ground in circumference surrounded with a rotten Stockade without a ditch, so defenceless that anyone can step in at pleasure." The barracks were "nothing more than miserable bark hutts, without any sort of Fire places or windows." [4]

Major Forbes found the paucity of townspeople distressing and was equally disturbed by the poor quality of those few persons who did make Pensacola their home. "At present," he wrote, "there are . . . but a few Settlers and followers of the Army, who more properly come under the Denomination of Pedlars than Merchants." Both officers commented unfavorably on the sandy nature of the soil, but they believed that "with great labour & a great deal of manure" the land might "produce vegetables." Colonel Prevost was encouraged when he discovered that "further back in the Country the land [was] good and capable of any Improvement." Furthermore, he wrote, the game was "extremely plenty in the Woods" and the sea was filled with "quantities of fish of different sorts & good." To Prevost's surprise, however, livestock was practically nonexistent.[5]

Although Mobile, with a population of some 350 people, was slightly larger than Pensacola, the British feared a sudden emigration of the townspeople. The French inhabitants, who comprised most of Mobile's population, were none too pleased with the prospect of British rule, and many were preparing to move to New Orleans, apparently under the impression that it would remain in French hands. As soon as they learned otherwise, all but a few elected to stay in Mobile rather than to live under the rule of Spaniards, whom they despised even more than they did the English. Major Robert Farmar, who accepted transfer of Mobile and its fortifications from the French on October 20, 1763, was distressed to find the fort in a dilapidated condition and the townspeople claiming most of the public buildings as their personal property. According to the chagrined Farmer, the French inhabitants claimed everything outside the fort, including "the hospital and magazine" which, they insisted, were "built at the King's expense." [6]

The only other area settled by Europeans in 1763 was along the eastern bank of the Mississippi River between Natchez and Manchac. While a few vestiges of French influence were evident to the careful observer, the region was still only sparsely inhabited when the British occupied it in 1764.[7] From an agricultural point of view, this portion of West Florida was much more promising than the barren coastal plains between Mobile and Pensacola. Located along the largest inland waterway in North America, this region also contained some of the richest soil on the continent. All British visitors to this part of West Florida were uniformly exuberant in their descriptions and were particularly enthusiastic about the area's potential value.

One of the earliest visitors was Montfort Browne, the colony's first lieutenant governor, who toured the western frontier in 1768 during his brief tenure as acting governor. Although his ecstatic comments are subject to suspicion since he wanted the British government to divide the province into two equal parts and appoint him governor of the western half, he did not greatly exaggerate when he described the Natchez District as one of "the most charming prospects in the world." He found the soil "exceeding fertile; consisting of black mould, at least three feet deep in the hills and much deeper in the bottoms" and the countryside filled with a bounteous supply of wild game and succulent fruit. "In all times of the year," Browne continued, "fish may be catched in the greatest abundance." He noted that from the fort at Natchez one could see "extensive plains intermixed with beautiful hills, and small rivers; here are . . . fruit Trees of most excellent kinds, the Grape, Peach, Plum, Apricot, Apple, Pear, Figs, Mulberry, Cherry, Persimmon, Medlars, and Strawberries as good in their kind as any in the world and in as great Abundance . . . . The Nut common in this part of the Province are Walnuts, Chestnuts, Hickory, and Filbert." [8]

Captain Philip Pittman toured the region in the late 1760s

in his capacity as an army officer, later publishing his recollections under the title *The Present State of European Settlements on the Mississippi.* In words reminiscent of Browne's, Pittman described the district as "the finest and most fertile part of West Florida" and promised his readers an unforgettable reward for climbing the steep bluff at Natchez. "The trouble of going up," he wrote, "is recompensed by the sight of a most delightful country of great extent, the prospect of which beautifully varied by a number of little hills and fine meadows." John H. Wynne, another British traveler during the same decade, echoed Pittman's sentiments in his *General History of the British Empire in America.* He seconded Browne's recommendation for establishing a separate colony at Natchez. "If we compare this [region] with the barren deserts of Canada and Florida," Wynne remarked, "what a wide difference is there." [9]

The second British official to visit the western frontier was Lieutenant Elias Durnford, who also served as surveyor general and councilor of the province. Touring the western district in 1771, Durnford thought the lands between the Mississippi and Pearl rivers were second to none in fertility and recommended that they be settled as soon as possible. "The Lands are capable of Producing the more valuable Commodity's," he reported in 1774 to Lord Dartmouth, Secretary of State for American affairs. "The soil in the Oak and Hicory Lands, is Black, or Brown Earth, with very little mixture of Sand, and the low River Lands are very fertile." [10]

Early settlers in the district were also good press agents, alerting friends and relatives in the more settled parts of the continent to the bright prospects of life on the southwestern frontier. Caleb Carpenter, one of Natchez's first merchants, believed the district contained "the most fertile, beautiful, healthy and variegated lands in this province, or perhaps in the whole continent of America." "They were," he declared, "watered by abundance of springs and rivulets, without swamps, and everywhere with spacious clearings, once old Indian fields, or French plantations." [11]

In spite of the prevailing belief that the fertile western part of the province would grow faster than the barren coastal plains between Mobile and Pensacola, the anticipated influx of settlers was slow to materialize. Several factors were responsible for this disappointing occurrence. In the first place, the seat of government, where justice was dispensed and land titles issued, was too far away to accommodate the needs of enterprising settlers. Communication between Pensacola and the Mississippi settlements was not only slow and difficult, but uncertain as well. Overland travel through dense underbrush and unfriendly Indian territory was all but impossible. The shortest water route was by means of the Iberville and Amite rivers, Lakes Maurepas and Pontchartrain, the Rigolets, and the Gulf of Mexico, but this too was extremely laborious and unsatisfactory, since the Iberville was never navigable for more than two or three months out of the year. The rest of the time the river was a dry bed of hard clay, punctured by thousands of small cracks. The British expected to overcome this problem by lowering the Iberville's bed and by removing the logs and other debris deposited there every spring when the Mississippi overflowed its banks. At least two British engineers drew up plans to make the river navigable the year around, but British officials failed, for one reason or another, to develop a stable water route for the region.

The only other way to reach the western settlements from the Gulf of Mexico was to proceed up the Mississippi River, but this route was even less satisfactory than the one through the lakes. The Spaniards controlled both banks of the Mississippi between Manchac and the Gulf including the valuable port of New Orleans, the only place where merchandise could be stored with relative ease. Although the Treaty of Paris guaranteed England free navigation of the Mississippi River, Spanish officials frequently held up British-owned vessels under some pretext and at other times seized them either for violating Spanish commercial laws or for engaging in illicit trade. Secondly, it was extremely time-consuming, if not impossible, for large vessels to proceed as far north as Natchez. The prevalence of sand bars at the Balize meant that only experienced pilots could navigate the treacherous waters of the Mississippi, and such men were in short supply. Unless the winds were blowing in the right direction, sails were worthless, and progress upstream was possible only through the more tedious methods of rowing or warping. In either case, travel was incredibly slow and very expensive.[12]

In addition to the problems associated with poor communications, the exposed western frontier also suffered from inadequate protection. Fortunately for the few hardy pioneers who braved the numerous adversities and moved to the Southwest after 1763, their closest neighbors—the Spaniards and the Choctaws—either were too weak to threaten them seriously or were willing to accept British occupation. Although the Spaniards were anxious to recover both Floridas, they were not strong enough to risk seizing them by force. The Choctaws who surrounded the English settlements on the eastern bank of the Mississippi remained on relatively good terms with the new settlers as long as the British continued to supply the Indians with provisions and did not intrude on their lands. British officials reluctantly agreed to provide the necessary supplies, and the paucity of European settlers prevented any serious intrusion on Indian territory. Nevertheless it was an

uneasy peace, and England's failure to provide western inhabitants with adequate protection kept the population from in-
creasing very rapidly.[13]

The failure of British officials in West Florida to respond
satisfactorily to the pleas of western inhabitants was not due
to ignorance or indifference, however. Every British governor
from George Johnstone to Peter Chester pleaded with officials
in London to supply the funds necessary to make the Iberville
navigable and to construct at least two forts along the Mississippi River, providing the troops required to garrison the forts
when they were completed. [14] Although Governor Johnstone
authorized the erection of Fort Bute just north of Manchac
at the confluence of the Iberville and Mississippi rivers and
the repairing of Fort Panmure, located on the high bluff at
Natchez where the French-built fort of Rosalie had previously
stood, economic considerations forced the British to abandon
these outposts in 1768. This pullback was part of a general
retrenchment program first suggested by Lord Shelburne and
later adopted by the ministry after the American colonists
violently objected to parliamentary taxes designed to defray
a portion of the high cost of defending the frontier. This
decision alarmed not only inhabitants of Natchez and Manchac but also officials at Pensacola, some of whom had already
received generous grants to lands between the Pearl and Mississippi rivers.[15]

As early as May, 1766, the governor of West Florida, with
approval of his council, began distributing lands along the
eastern bank of the Mississippi to veterans of the Seven Years'
War who qualified under the provisions of the Proclamation
Act of 1763 and to immigrants and court favorites under authority of the royal mandamus or upon instructions from the
Board of Trade in London. For the most part, the earliest

grants of land in the Natchez District were large, varying in size from 140 to 20,000 acres and were given more often to prominent political figures than to actual settlers. Although all grants were conditioned upon improvements being made on the lands, only a few of these early grantees ever attempted to comply with these provisions or to settle the additional colonists as required by law. A few individuals and families, however, did settle on their lands. Daniel Clark, Sr., who later became one of the district's most prominent planters, received title to 3,000 acres in 1767, and John Blommart, one of Natchez's earliest and most successful merchants, obtained 1,000 acres. John Bradley and Henry Fairchild, who together operated the only trading post at Natchez before 1770, were each given 1,000 acres in 1767. The largest grants, however, went to prominent Englishmen. Among the earliest claimants were wealthy London merchant Samuel Hannay, who received 5,000 acres, and the Earl of Eglinton, whose 20,000 acres placed him in a category all by himself.[16]

Since most grantees never bothered to improve their lands, the western extremity of the province contained but a few permanent residents until 1770, when a noticeable spurt in growth commenced. Despite the failure of Great Britain to provide the district with adequate protection, the fertility of the soil was too inviting to deter the more hardy pioneers. The Mississippi River acted as a convenient highway, attracting English settlers from the North, and it also provided planters with a suitable outlet for their surplus produce.

The hazardous nature of travel to the Southwest encouraged immigrants to come in groups rather than alone. Although a single family sometimes braved the elements and came by itself, large parties were more commonplace. Since land and timber were in greater supply than labor, most newcomers brought slaves with them or purchased them along the way either from dealers in New Orleans or from established planters in British West Florida. Consequently, the western region quickly took on a few features of antebellum southern plantation society even while it was an undeveloped frontier.[17]

Large migrations to the western part of the province began as early as 1770. In that year, a number of Virginians sent an agent by the name of Holt to survey lands along the Mississippi in hopes of settling there later. In its meeting of May 1, 1770, the Council of West Florida approved Lieutenant Governor Durnford's recommendation to reserve for Holt and his associates a ten-mile strip of land along the eastern bank of the Mississippi. In June, a boatload of Marylanders, destined for the Natchez region but unfamiliar with the perplexing Louisiana coastline, missed the mouth of the Mississippi and were finally forced to land at the port of Espíritu Santo where the Spaniards confiscated their property.[18]

More successful was a party of seventy-nine whites and eighteen blacks from Pennsylvania and Virginia who arrived at Natchez in July of 1770 after a long trip down the Ohio and Mississippi rivers from Fort Pitt. Their safe journey was partly the result of a fortuitous meeting at the mouth of the Muskingum River with Daniel Huay, a skilled river pilot, who safely guided them the rest of the way. Huay agreed to accompany the expedition to Natchez in expectation of locating some choice lands where he might also settle permanently. In addition to the usual number of enterprising farmers, the group also included a few carpenters and blacksmiths, and John McIntire, leader of the Pennsylvanians, brought along enough equipment to erect a sawmill and a gristmill.

Although the immigrants arrived at a poor time (the Indians a few months earlier having almost destroyed the fort), Huay was so impressed with the land that he agreed to proceed immediately to Pensacola. Armed with a letter from McIntire, Huay reached Pensacola in late August and inquired about the terms upon which land was granted and about the prospects of extending protection to the exposed region. If the British provided some form of security, Huay assured Governor Chester, a hundred families would come from North Carolina alone. McIntire, in his letter, estimated that an equal number of families from the back country of Pennsylvania and Virginia waited only for a favorable word from the governor before proceeding to Natchez.[19]

Encouraged by this trickle of newcomers in 1770, Governor Chester and the West Florida Council took positive steps the following year to promote further migrations to the western part of the province. At its August meeting of 1771, the council authorized John Thomas, a justice of the peace and Indian commissary at Manchac, to take affidavits from immigrants, thereby relieving them of the necessity of a long journey to Pensacola in order to register their claims. A few months later, the council allowed the provincial surveyor to appoint persons who resided along the Mississippi as his deputies, an action which further reduced the cost of acquiring land. In response to a request from Colonel John Clark, who represented some 200 families on the Holston River, the council also agreed partially to subsidize newcomers to the province by providing each of them with a barrel of corn a month and a proportionate amount of salt until the settlers were able to support themselves.[20]

These new policies seemingly had the desired effect for the number of petitions for lands in the Southwest increased significantly. In April, 1772, the council received ten petitions for town lots in Manchac alone. In October, this same body granted Captain Amos Ogden 25,000 acres near Natchez and reserved for those New Jersey families scheduled to accompany him an additional strip of 15,000 acres along the Mississippi River. Although Ogden was unable to attract the necessary number of settlers, he sold 19,000 acres to another group from New Jersey, headed by Richard and Samuel Swayze. By late 1772, the Swayze brothers had successfully planted a settlement on the Homochitto River southeast of Natchez. Most of these immigrants had been members of Samuel Swayze's Congregational Church in New Jersey and had followed their minister to the Southwest. Of all the early colonizing efforts, the "Jersey settlement" was the most successful.[21]

Larger in scope but less successful in operation than the Swayze project was one planned by a number of New England veterans of the Seven Years' War, most of whom were from Connecticut. Thwarted in earlier efforts to obtain lands in the Ohio Valley, these promoters turned their attention to the Southwest where General Phineas Lyman, principal agent for the group, had personally received 25,000 acres in 1770. Representing an organization called the Company of Military Adventurers, Colonel Israel Putnam, who was later to distinguish himself in the American Revolution, and three associates appeared before the council in March of 1773. They were in West Florida, Putnam explained, to reserve certain lands along the Mississippi in anticipation of grants they expected to receive shortly from the Crown. In fact, General Lyman had been in London for several years seeking, without much success, an extensive western land grant for the company. The council gladly allowed the four commissioners to select suitable tracts of choice lands south of Natchez and went so far as to assure them that, even if the royal grant failed to materialize, they could still receive the property on the same basis as other settlers. Although the council reserved for the company nineteen townships of approximately 23,000 acres each, those who settled there in 1774 received a severe jolt when the British government in late 1773 put a temporary halt to its previous policy of allowing governors in the least settled provinces to grant lands freely.[22]

Before this alarming development occurred, however, Governor Chester and his council had already made extensive grants to several groups of potential immigrants in return for promises to settle a certain number of families on the fertile lands along the eastern bank of the Mississippi. In April, 1773, Garrett Rapalje of New York and his associates were promised 25,000 acres. In June, Thomas Hutchins and associates also received 25,000 acres near Natchez, provided their claim did not conflict in any way with that previously given the Company of Military Adventurers. In June, grants of a similiar size were made to Peter Van Brugh Livingston, a kinsman of provincial secretary Philip Livingston, and his associates and to two Pensacola merchants, James and Evon Jones, and their associates. Two weeks later, Colonel Anthony Hutchins, Thomas's older brother, and his associates were reserved a tract of 152,000 acres upon which the grantees agreed to settle families from Virginia and the Carolinas.[23]

While only a few of the large grantees fulfilled all or even part of the requirements to settle families on their extensive reservations, this generous policy nevertheless stimulated settlement even under the most adverse of conditions. In late 1773, however, the British ministry abruptly ordered an end to the policy of free grants. In early 1774 Lord Dartmouth, colonial secretary for the American colonies, announced a new procedure. Henceforth, unappropriated lands were first to be surveyed into numbered lots, ranging in size from 100 to 1,000 acres, and then, after a six-months' notice, were to be publicly auctioned off at a minimum price of sixpence an acre. In an effort to minimize the adverse effects of this change, the governor and council unanimously agreed that all settlers presently in the province without grants of land as well as those who might arrive in the future should be allowed to settle on unoccupied lands and be given the right to claim these same lands at a later date in case England returned to its earlier policy.[24]

Although the ban on granting free lands to actual settlers raised serious questions about the extensive claims of the Company of Military Adventurers, since half of that group's huge reservation was based upon family rights, 104 families, averaging between six and eight persons to a household, were already in West Florida or on their way there, and an additional 300 families were contemplating a move to the Natchez District. On March 5, 1774, Major Timothy Hierlichy and four other agents of the company petitioned the council to recognize their claims since their grant had actually been consummated prior to the change in policy. Always anxious to promote additional settlement, the council, not knowing what else to do, referred the memorial to the colonial secretary in London and urged him to act favorably on it. In July, 1774, Lord Dartmouth replied that since the king's new plan for disposing of lands in North America would "not admit any indulgence" he could only "lament the Disappointment they will feel upon the Occasion." [25]

Even without the certainty of securing titles to the land, settlers continued to arrive and to cultivate vacant lands in hopes of legally acquiring them later. Since British officials never took an accurate census of the province, the exact number of settlers can only be surmised. In early 1774, Lieutenant

Governor Durnford offered his account of the western district in a brief report to the ministry. According to Durnford, approximately thirty to forty families, several of whom held "considerable property in slaves" and one of whom possessed "no less than 80 working slaves," resided in the region by the end of 1772. During the next year, at least 150 additional families arrived to swell the number of inhabitants to "no less than 2,500 whites and 600 slaves" (apparently there were no free blacks or mulattoes). The settlers had come into the province "not only by sea, from New England, New York, Georgia & East Florida but [also] by the River Ohio, from the Back Settlements of Maryland, Virginia, & Carolinas." [26] Largely due to an influx of New Englanders in 1774, the next year saw no serious abatement in the number of new arrivals despite the change in land policy. By the outbreak of the American Revolution, the western extremity of the province contained a population considerably larger than that of the eastern portion, where settlement during the 1770s had not kept pace largely because the expected increase in commerce with the West Indies had not occurred.

In recognition of this disparity in growth, the council quickly extended to westerners certain conveniences previously enjoyed by their eastern counterparts. In the spring of 1774, Mississippi settlers petitioned for and were granted a court of common pleas to hear civil cases and a court of requests to facilitate the collection of small debts. In response to another complaint, Governor Chester agreed to appoint a second English pilot at the mouth of the Mississippi and further acceded to the demands of the petitioners by selecting John Selkeld to the newly created post.[27]

By 1775, the western sector of the province consisted of four well-defined centers of settlement. In contrast to the eastern part of West Florida where most of the population lived in towns, western settlements were less concentrated. All but a few of the inhabitants resided in scattered rural communities. The northernmost cluster of settlers was located around Natchez where the rich soil and cleared lands attracted a host of immigrants. These settlers generally owned their own lands and usually brought black slaves with them or hired free white laborers to cultivate the soil. A small, motley collection of individuals took up residence at the landing. Above the landing, on the Natchez bluff, stood the dilapidated and abandoned Fort Panmure, a welcome landmark for weary travelers coming down the Mississippi River. In 1776, when the British officially laid out a town at Natchez, the settlement contained only "ten log houses and two frame houses" in addition to the deserted fort.[28]

Even with only this small beginning, the growing community's commercial needs were extensive enough by the end of 1776 to support four merchants. The two newest mercantile establishments were owned by men whose later fame would transcend the field of commerce. John Blommart, a former British army captain who was blessed with a lifetime pension of half-pay, operated a small but profitable enterprise where he also retailed the bottled products of two stills, one of which had a capacity of 160 gallons. Possessing an impressive library of 150 volumes, Blommart was the district's resident intellectual and one of its leading citizens. James Willing, whose name was later to be indelibly etched in the annals of Southwestern history, ran a less successful mercantile venture, but his personal connection with the prominent Philadelphia families of his brother Thomas and Robert Morris assured him a place in the social life of the Southwest. Unfortunately, he devoted more time to enjoying the pleasures of that relationship than to advancing his business interest, and he failed to take advantage of the numerous opportunities available in the rapidly changing frontier environment.[29]

But agriculture more than commerce dominated the life of this small community. In addition to raising a variety of fruits and vegetables necessary to sustain life in the frontier outpost, some of the early settlers also produced a few staples for export. The larger planters grew tobacco and indigo; these with raw timber, lumber, and barrel staves constituted the region's only principal exports. Profits from these products were large enough by 1778 to allow a few individuals to import such luxuries as cognac, Madeira, port, and fine linens.[30]

Approximately 100 miles south of Natchez was the smaller settlement of New Richmond or Baton Rouge as it came to be called because of the reddish tinge of the cypress trees in the vicinity. Except for the smaller number of settlers residing there, lands in the Baton Rouge area closely resembled those at Natchez. They too were "very beautiful and fertile." A dozen or so planters, owning fairly extensive claims along the eastern bank of the Mississippi and holding a large number of Negro slaves, cultivated a variety of crops, including sizable quantities of corn, rice, indigo, and tobacco, a small amount of cotton, and the usual assortment of garden vegetables. In addition they raised cattle and hogs. Except for the lands adjacent to Brown's Cliff, just south of where Thompson's Creek emptied into the Mississippi, a large cypress swamp, which in places was a quarter of a mile wide, separated these settlements from the river, making transportation difficult and life unpleasant.[31]

Although Governor Montfort Browne received two gigantic grants of land in the area (one a 17,000-acre tract and the other 10,000 acres), he held them primarily for speculation and rented out only enough acreage to satisfy the conditions of his grants. His principal leasee was a successful planter named Francis Poussette.

In many ways, the most remarkable resident at Baton Rouge was William Dunbar, youngest son of a Scottish nobleman who migrated to the Southwest after spending two years in western Pennsylvania. Other prominent area settlers included Stephen Watts, Samuel Flowers, George Castles, William Marshall, and James Willing who owned lands along Bayou Tunica, which at that time was usually referred to as Willing's Bayou. The fact that Willing was both a Baton Rouge planter and a Natchez merchant and that Dunbar lived most of his later life in Natchez is indicative of the close connections, both economically and socially, which existed between the two settlements. Nor was Dunbar the only settler to own lands on both sides of the river. Across the Mississippi River and just to the north of Baton Rouge stood the larger and more prosperous Spanish town of Pointe Coupée, whose presence may account for the slow growth of English settlements on the eastern bank which as late as 1785 contained only 270 inhabitants.[32]

The southernmost British settlement along the Mississippi was Manchac. There the English had erected Fort Bute which they temporarily abandoned in 1768. By the outbreak of the American Revolution, the fort had fallen into disrepair. In contrast to Natchez and Baton Rouge where farming communities sprang up, Manchac was primarily a commercial and strategic post. Located near the confluence of the Iberville (later Bayou Manchac) and the Mississippi rivers, Manchac was the vital link between the western agricultural settlements along the Mississippi and the commercial centers of Mobile and Pensacola on the Gulf. British officials considered

Manchac so important to the future growth of West Florida that Lieutenant Governor Durnford and Governor Chester even recommended, at different times, transferring the provincial capital there. Yet Manchac's potential would not be realized until the British lowered the bed of the Iberville River and made it navigable the year around.[33]

In the meantime, Manchac remained a small trading post. When famous English botanist William Bartram visited the town in 1773, he found a few "large and commodious" buildings, including "the warehouses of Messrs. Swanson & Co. Indian traders and merchants." John Fitzpatrick, the most successful merchant in Manchac, functioned as an important middleman, supplying local planters on both sides of the river as far north as the Arkansas with manufactured goods which he purchased usually from the larger trading companies in Pensacola or Mobile, and occasionally from firms in New Orleans. Fitzpatrick sometimes handled similar transactions for fur traders and small merchants in the Illinois country. Because of the scarcity of specie, he was often forced to accept as payment carrots of tobacco, indigo, corn or other agricultural products which he in turn used to satisfy his own creditors in Mobile, Pensacola, and New Orleans.

Although the British laid out the town of Harwick just north of Manchac in 1775 and began granting lots in 1777, it never developed into a flourishing community, disappearing entirely after the Spaniards seized the region in 1779. As a precautionary measure, the Spaniards also established a small fort, garrisoned by a few soldiers, on the southern bank of the Iberville across from Manchac. "A slender narrow, wooden bridge . . . supported on wooden pillars" made travel possible between the two settlements during the winter and spring months when the otherwise dry bed of the Iberville River turned into "a very rapid stream." [34]

The only other settled area in the western part of the province was located east of Manchac and north of Lake Pontchartrain along the lower end of the Amite River. Lands in this region were not as fertile as those along the Mississippi, causing the Amite settlement to lag somewhat behind Natchez and Baton Rouge in population. Futhermore, those immigrants coming to the province by way of the Mississippi River usually stopped before they reached the Spanish border and therefore did not consider the possibility of settling along the Amite River or on the northern shores of Lakes Pontchartrain and Maurepas.

In 1773, when William Bartram visited the region on his way to the Mississippi settlements, he found the countryside rich in timber and in fruit trees of many descriptions. He noted that the northern shore of the lakes between the Pearl and Amite rivers was sprinkled with a few inhabitants. Bartram especially enjoyed the hospitality of James Rumsey who lived alone on the beautiful island of Pearl near the mouth of the river by the same name. The botanist stayed there several days until he recovered from an illness and was strong enough to endure once more the rigors of traveling.[35]

West of the British settlements along the Mississippi River lay the more populous province of Louisiana. Although ruled by Spain during the American Revolution, most of Louisiana's inhabitants were French or German in origin. In large measure, this population pattern reflected the fact that France had not only settled Louisiana in the late seventeeth century but had also controlled it during the first sixty years of the eighteenth century. The German element in the province had been settled there by France in a desperate effort to attract population. Although originally destined for the upper reaches of the province, the Germans became dissatisfied and drifted south, settling finally along both banks of the Mississippi River a few miles north of New Orleans. This settlement, which became known as the German Coast, contained approximately 2,600 people by 1777.[36]

The cultural and commercial center of Louisiana was New Orleans, located on the east side of the Mississippi River roughly halfway between the Gulf of Mexico and British Manchac. When Governor Bernardo de Gálvez took a census in May of 1777, the population of New Orleans was 3,202. Situated on the Island of Orleans which was completely surrounded by water only when the Mississippi overflowed its banks and filled the Iberville River, the city of New Orleans was surrounded by swampy and uninhabitable lands. Nevertheless, settlements sprang up intermittently along both banks of the Mississippi beginning about thirty miles from the sea and extending as far north as Manchac. A few miles south of the Iberville River was a settlement of some 1,300 Acadians who were originally from Nova Scotia. Between the Balize on the south and the German Coast on the north, an additional 5,000 inhabitants lived along the Mississippi River in settlements outside the city limits of New Orleans.

Along the western bank of the Mississippi north of the Iberville, settlements were more scattered and smaller in size. A thriving community of 1,600 people existed at Pointe Coupée, opposite the much smaller English settlement of the same name. Farther to the north were the tiny settlements around the Arkansas Post where less than a hundred people lived and the more scattered outposts in the western part of the Illinois country where some 1,500 hardy souls eked out a living. Farther to the west were a few isolated pockets of European population, the largest being at Opelousas, Attakapas, and Natchitoches, but these distant settlements posed no serious threat to British residents along the Mississippi.

The total population of Louisiana was more than 17,000, much larger than that of West Florida, but the British settlements were growing at a much faster rate during the 1770s than were the Spanish ones. Although the western side of the river was just as fertile as the eastern bank and although Louisiana's natural resources were as plentiful as those in West Florida, the Spanish province lacked a permanent outlet for its products. In contrast to British West Florida which traded heavily with England and her New World colonies, especially those in the West Indies, Louisiana was too dependent upon uncertain foreign markets. Furthermore, the non-Spanish inhabitants of the province remained suspicious of their Spanish rulers. Consequently, the internal weakness of Louisiana largely negated the numerical superiority of her population and forced Spanish officials in New Orleans and Madrid to move warily in their dealings with the British in Pensacola and London.[37]

The Mississippi River and Lakes Pontchartrain and Maurepas divided British West Florida from Spanish Louisiana, but no such natural boundaries separated English settlers from the various Indian tribes who inhabited the forests to the north and east of the Natchez District. Three important southern tribes claimed lands contiguous to British West Florida. To the north of Pensacola and Mobile was the loosely connected confederation of Creek Indians who resided in present-day southeastern Alabama. Subdivided into the Upper Creeks and the Lower Creeks, they were the most faction-ridden of the three southern tribes and therefore the least dependable from the British point of view.

To the west of the Creeks and to the east of Natchez were the Choctaws, residing in the territory between the Tombigbee and Pearl rivers in what is now southern Mississippi.

Although more united than the Creeks, they too were divided into three principal groups—East Party, West Party, and Six Towns. The Choctaws were generally friendly toward the British, although they sometimes accepted favors from the Spaniards, a policy which prevented England from taking them for granted.

The smallest of the three major tribes in the Old Southwest was the Chickasaw nation, whose warriors hunted in the lands to the north of the Choctaw. The principal towns of this tribe were located in the northern part of present-day Mississippi. Of all the southern Indians, the Chickasaws were the most favorably inclined toward England, even though great distances separated their villages from the trading towns of Pensacola and Mobile, where they received gifts from their European allies. Because of the Chickasaw's unshakable loyalty to England, British officials in West Florida came to rely heavily upon their goodwill during the trying period of the American Revolution.[38]

2

A Loyalist Outpost

WHEN the American Revolution broke out in April of 1775, inhabitants in and around the small trading post of Natchez were far removed from the scene of initial hostilities and, for the most part, were unconcerned with the issues which had provoked the disturbance. Although the controversies that triggered the rebellion centered primarily in New England and secondarily in Virginia, all thirteen English colonies represented in the Second Continental Congress were affected in one way or another. An entirely different set of problems, however, occupied the attention of that small but hearty band of pioneers who inhabited the Natchez District. By sheer necessity, these settlers were concerned primarily with surviving and not with the questions of local rights or individual liberties as were the inhabitants of the more mature and more densely populated colonies to the northeast. In late 1775, Governor Peter Chester of West Florida proudly informed his superiors in London, "We are in a State of great Tranquility here, and I am happy to say that the Inhabitants of this Colony are well attached to the Constitution." [1]

Despite Chester's optimism, the rebellious situation in the eastern colonies troubled him and the other British officials in Pensacola. While the governor was satisfied that the citizens of West Florida disapproved of these developments, the "unhappy State of Government" in the nearby colonies of South Carolina and Georgia still made him uneasy. The news of Superintendent John Stuart's hasty departure from Charleston ahead of an angry mob of American rebels who were intent upon punishing Stuart for having induced the Indians "to fall upon the back Inhabitants of the Provinces" was particularly alarming. Although he was convinced that the charges against Stuart were groundless and that his sudden flight was justified under the circumstances, Governor Chester still feared that the superintendent's behavior might encourage the Indians to undertake aggressive action against exposed English settlers in West Florida.[2]

Chester became even more apprehensive when in June, 1775, General Thomas Gage, commanding general of British forces in North America, reduced the size of the garrison at Pensacola by withdrawing three companies of the Sixteenth Regiment. The governor felt that Gage's decision, combined with the poor state of defenses at Pensacola and the uncertainty of receiving the necessary Indian presents, made the province disturbingly vulnerable to attack should any or all of the three principal southern tribes—Creeks, Choctaws, Chickasaws—switch allegiance from England to the American rebels. Chester was also worried over the prospect of war with Spain, since that nation controlled not only Louisiana but also several large islands in the Caribbean. From any of her bases in these areas, she could easily molest British shipping in the Gulf of Mexico or, even worse, launch a massive attack against West Florida. The governor realized that if a foreign war occurred, Florida would surely fall to Spanish arms without the timely assistance of friendly Indians. Chester could only hope for a speedy end to the calamitous conditions in the other

North American colonies before the contagion had a chance to spread into the Southwest.[3]

The immediate effects of the American Revolution in West Florida were not all bad since the disturbances in the eastern colonies stimulated a new wave of immigration into the province. Taking advantage of the ministry's decision to rescind its earlier order suspending all land grants in North America, Governor Chester on November 11, 1775, announced his intention of making West Florida "a secure Asylum" for "the well affected Inhabitants of the rebellious colonies" who were "too weak to resist the violence of the times and too loyal to concur in the measures of those who had avowed and supported that Rebellion." The governor promised all immigrants who could provide him with "good evidence of their loyalty" generous grants of land not to exceed 1,000 acres per household. He offered 100 acres of land to "the master or mistress" of each family as well as 50 additional acres to "every [other] white or black man, woman, or child" in the same household. Heads of family who could demonstrate a "firm attachment to the Constitution" and who had "suffered considerably on that account," might receive as much as 3,000 acres provided they submitted proof of their ability to cultivate that much land.[4]

In an effort to assist potential immigrants in overcoming transportation difficulties, Chester tried, without success, to persuade the British government to take the travelers to West Florida on the same ships that brought troops from England to the colonies. Before returning home, Chester suggested, these ships could transport colonists to Mobile and Pensacola or even to the Mississippi settlements. The governor also reminded Lord Dartmouth of the potential advantages to the

British empire from developing West Florida into a prosperous colony. If the rebellion lasted longer than expected, as many were beginning to think it might, the West Indies would be forced to look elsewhere for lumber and foodstuffs, and West Florida was the most likely source for these supplies. Chester noted that "the Quantity of Excellent Timber in [the] colony" was "almost inexhaustable," and corn also grew in abundance. Although by late 1775 the number of persons who had fled the disturbances in eastern areas and settled in West Florida was small, Chester felt that there were "many thousand Loyal Subjects in different colonies anxious to follow their example." As an inducement for attracting more settlers, Chester recommended providing the more destitute with a few essential farm implements, and the next year Parliament appropriated the necessary funds to comply with the governor's suggestion.[5]

As a result of these new British endeavors, immigration to the more fertile western parts of the province picked up perceptibly after 1776. In the forefront of this new flood of settlers were American Loyalists escaping disorders in the older English colonies and individuals who preferred to remain neutral but who feared they could not do so if they stayed where they were. Although some were without property of any sort, most of the newcomers were fairly substantial citizens and a number brought along sizable holdings of slaves and livestock.

The refugees came from practically every colony in British North America and from a few islands in the Caribbean. However, the southern colonies, especially Georgia and South Carolina, contributed the bulk of these newcomers. A typical settler was Bernard Lintot, who brought his wife, seven children, two indentured servants, and seven black slaves with him when he came from Connecticut in late 1775, just in time to take advantage of Chester's proclamation. Among the immigrants arriving during the summer of 1776 were two slaveholders from Georgia—Thomas Bassett, who brought along fourteen slaves, and William Webb, accompanied by five black servants. The following summer William Marshall with twenty slaves and David Holmes with twenty-two blacks migrated from South Carolina. From the same state came Alexander Graiden, a skilled carpenter, and two apprentices.[6]

At least two large parties of immigrants journeyed to the province during the early years of the American Revolution. Beginning in early 1776, a group of Virginia Loyalists settled along the eastern bank of the Pearl River where they received extensive grants of land. Most of them were modest slaveholders, owning from one to ten blacks each. Larger in size was a colony of approximately forty whites and five hundred slaves from South Carolina, apparently led by John Turner, who in 1778 settled near Natchez. According to Governor Chester, many of the South Carolinians were "Men of Property and Influence in Carolina" and a few had been severe critics of the British government until they became disgusted with the tactics of the more militant patriots and refused to support the cause of independence.[7]

At least one of the newcomers bore an illustrious colonial name. He was Thomas Taylor Byrd, son of the late Colonel William Byrd of Westover in Virginia. After hearing how the younger Byrd had suffered severely for his support of the king, the council rewarded him with a grant of 1,100 acres of land. The council was even more generous in the case of James Baird, a North Carolinian who arrived with a tale of woe similar to Byrd's and with a mandamus for membership on the council. Baird received a warrant for 1,900 acres. Among several Pennsylvanians who arrived between 1776 and

1778 were Christian Buckler and William Hiorn, both of whom quickly gained the respect of settlers in their respective communities.

Although the British never took an accurate census of West Florida during the American Revolution, the population of the western half of the province almost doubled between 1775 and 1779, and by the end of the decade the number of settlers in this part of West Florida far surpassed those in the eastern districts. Among the western settlers, the black population increased at an even faster rate than the white. The influx of immigrants also raised the social level of the settlements since many of the newcomers were from the upper and middle classes of colonial society, as suggested by the large number of slaves they brought with them.[8]

For the most part, the recent immigrants had no difficulty blending in with the older residents who were busily trying to transform an unspoiled wilderness into the garden paradise of their dreams. Although most of the newer inhabitants followed the course of the American Revolution more closely than did the earlier settlers, they usually kept these personal feelings to themselves and were careful not to upset the peace and tranquility of the district which the sanctuary of distance afforded them and which was their prime reason for being there in the first place.

As American resistance stiffened and as British determination to suppress the colonial rebellion hardened during late 1775 and early 1776, Governor Chester grew more and more fearful that the fighting might spread into the Southwest. The American decision in July of 1776 to declare independence only served to reinforce these fears. The principal reason for Chester's uneasiness was the numerous reports of a projected American invasion of West Florida which littered his desk.

The governor called the West Florida Council together in early May, 1776, after the schooner *Sally* arrived from Jamaica with news that the Americans were massing "between six and seven thousand troops, upon the River Ohio with intent to attack this province." [9]

The first proof that Chester's fears were more than imaginary came in the fall of 1776, when a British merchant in New Orleans informed British officials in Pensacola that an American captain had arrived in that city from Pennsylvania, that the governor of Louisiana had received him "civilly," and that one of the captain's associates had returned upstream with a sizable quantity of powder for the American rebels.[10] Subsequent intelligence from other sources confirmed the accuracy of this sketchy report, and filled in most of the details.

Armed with letters of introduction from Major General Charles Lee, commanding officer of the Southern District, and from the Virginia Committee of Safety, Captain George Gibson, disguised as a trader and accompanied by "eighteen Men and a Boy," set out in a barge from Fort Pitt.[11] In early August, the party stopped briefly at Walnut Hills (modern Vicksburg) where two or three of its members "openly declared that they were on their way to New Orleans, charged by the Philadelphia Congress with despatches for the Court of Spain and the Governor of Louisiana." Gibson confided to the local magistrate that "part of his business was to open trade between Louisiana and the United States." When Gibson's boat passed by Natchez on its way to New Orleans, inhabitants along the bank watched as the Americans "hoisted the Rebel colours." [12]

Before delivering the letters to Spanish Governor Luis de Unzaga y Amezaga as he was instructed, Captain Gibson contacted Oliver Pollock, an influential New Orleans merchant of Irish extraction and an ardent patriot whose "soul panted

for the success of American arms." Pollock had first come to
New Orleans in 1768 shortly before his friend and fellow
Irishman Alejandro O'Reilly arrived in Louisiana at the head
of a Spanish army. O'Reilly had been sent to suppress a rebellion among the French inhabitants and to assume governor-
ship of the province. When a famine threatened to engulf the
colony after the cost of flour suddenly shot up to thirty dollars
a barrel, Pollock further cemented his friendship with the new
governor by agreeing to sell him a cargo of the precious white
gold at half the prevailing price. Out of a sense of gratitude,
O'Reilly extended to the American merchant freedom of trade
in Louisiana, a privilege which Pollock, who spoke Spanish
fluently, continued to enjoy as long as he remained in the
Southwest.[13]

Just before O'Reilly left Louisiana, he introduced Pollock
to his successor, Governor Unzaga, and the close ties between
the American merchant and the Spanish governor remained
unbroken. "During the whole of his government," Pollock
stated later, "I supplied the country frequently with provisions, dry goods, and Negroes." According to one keen observer of affairs in that part of the continent, "Mr Pollock's
connection with the Spanish officers, at New Orleans, was the
most intimate, and his influence boundless, from the administration of Governor O'Reilly to that of Governor Miro." [14]

Through contact with some of Pollock's relatives in the
Cumberland Valley, Captain Gibson was thoroughly familiar
with the American's favored position in New Orleans, and he
took advantage of this situation to secure a personal audience
with the Spanish governor. Dressed as a "humbly-clad citizen," Gibson was escorted to the governor's house where he
candidly discussed with Unzaga the purpose of his secret mission. Gibson explained that the Americans were in dire need

of certain articles of trade which Spain was in a position to supply. He specifically mentioned muskets, powder, blankets, and "medicinal drugs particularly quinine," which the Americans had heretofore obtained from England or the British West Indies. In response to Gibson's special plea for gunpowder, Unzaga "privately delivered" some 10,000 pounds from the king's store to Pollock, who in turn handed it over to Gibson. To pay for the powder, Gibson drew a draft of "One thousand Eight Hundred and Fifty Spanish mill'd Dollars" on the "Grand Council of Virginia." [15]

Even though the cautious Unzaga agreed surreptitiously to assist the Americans, Gibson's presence in New Orleans, brief as it was, made the Spanish governor visibly uneasy. Anxious to maintain the appearance of neutrality, he feared—correctly as it turned out—that British spies might learn of his activities and protest to his superiors in Madrid. In an effort to keep these transactions as secret as possible and to give England no cause for alarm, Unzaga had Gibson submit to arrest for a brief period of time while Lieutenant William Linn left for Fort Pitt with 9,000 pounds of gunpowder on board a batteau flying the colors of Spain and with a Spanish master at the helm.

Equally troublesome to the wary governor were Gibson's inquiries about the state of defenses at Pensacola and Mobile and his declaration that a large force of Americans planned "to descend the river next spring . . . in order to lay waste and seize the land occupied by various Englishmen living between Manchak . . . and the river called Ohio." Gibson made it abundantly clear that the final objective of the expedition was the capture of Mobile and Pensacola. Assisting the Americans to fight England along the Atlantic coast was one thing, but encouraging them to send troops down the Mississippi

River and thereby inviting possible British retaliation was something else. In a carefully worded message to José de Gálvez, minister of the Indies, Unzaga outlined the purpose of Gibson's visit and detailed his own apprehensions about the potential threat which the United States posed to Spanish control of Louisiana and Mexico. Meanwhile Unzaga refused Gibson's request to open up trade with the American rebels on a regular basis until he had received specific authorization to that effect from the king, and he urged officials in Madrid to provide him with an armed frigate to prevent a surprise attack from the north by way of the Mississippi River.

Gálvez and other Spanish officials, however, viewed these proceedings with less foreboding. After giving the official stamp of approval to Unzaga's previous actions, Gálvez told the governor that if the Americans persisted in their desire to seize British West Florida he was to inform them "that the King [would] be glad to see them succeed." In the meantime, Unzaga was to "obtain through Havana and by as many other ways, aid in arms, ammunition, clothing, and quinine asked for by the English colonies" although he was cautioned to use "the most prudent and secret methods." Unzaga was to channel all assistance through "private traders," preferably through someone willing "to be used as a stool pigeon." By late 1776, the identity of the individual Gálvez had in mind was obvious; it was Oliver Pollock.[16]

Gibson's visit to New Orleans turned out to be remarkably successful. The only remaining question was whether the United States was willing and strong enough to take advantage of the possibilities which Gibson had uncovered by dislodging the British from forts along the Mississippi River. The disadvantages of relying too heavily upon the Mississippi trade, however, were borne out by the hardships Lieutenant

Linn and his men experienced in transporting the supplies upstream to Fort Pitt. On September 22, Linn and forty-three other men left New Orleans with 9,000 pounds of gunpowder in a vessel purchased specifically for that purpose by Pollock. By the time they reached the Arkansas River in late November, the men were "almost half dead" from the arduous labor of rowing upstream. Linn reported that every night half the oarsmen were so exhausted that the others had to carry them "in Blankets to the fire" or else help them "to walk out" of the boats. Consequently Linn, with consent of the Spanish commandant, decided to spend the winter at the Arkansas Post. While the men passed the time hunting wild animals for their meat, Linn arranged to purchase two thousand dollars worth of provisions for which he paid by drawing more drafts on Pollock. With the approach of spring, Linn again set out for Fort Pitt, arriving there with the powder in late April just in time to save that post and another at Wheeling from falling into enemy hands.[17]

Despite the elaborate precautions taken by Unzaga and Pollock to conceal the aid furnished to Gibson, the British uncovered almost every detail of the transaction. Merchant John Fitzpatrick saw Linn's batteau when it passed Manchac and heard that it contained several thousand pounds of gunpowder. "She never called here going up or down," Fitzpatrick reported sadly. When the boat finally stopped farther upstream, the Spanish captain explained to the inhabitants that he was going north to trade with Indians in Spanish territory and that he had hired the "North Americans to assist in rowing his batteau." Although Superintendent Stuart tried to prevail upon the Chickasaws to intercept the vessel before it reached the Ohio River, they refused to comply since it would interfere with their hunting season.[18]

British spies in New Orleans and Philadelphia also furnished Governor Chester with information on the subsequent movements of Captain Gibson. Shortly after Linn was safely out of Louisiana, Unzaga released Gibson from confinement. Pollock then arranged for Gibson and Captain George Ord, who had recently lost his ship to a British sloop of war, to secure passage to Philadelphia on a vessel registered to the prominent American firm of Willing and Morris, whose owners were close friends of Pollock. Pollock also managed to place on board the ship "thirty-nine pipes of gunpowder." In early November, Gibson, Ord, and the munitions, together with some secret dispatches for Congress, arrived safely in Philadelphia. This intelligence caused Governor Chester to conclude that the Continental Congress had sent Gibson south not only to negotiate for supplies, but also to learn of "our Strength, disposition of the back Inhabitants, Quantities of Provisions, and the difficulties attending an Expedition against that Quarter." [19]

In early November, 1777, Governor Chester lodged a formal complaint with Governor Unzaga. Although he believed that Unzaga was deeply involved in the affair, Chester refrained from accusing him of personally providing the Americans with military supplies. Instead he took the position that some of Unzaga's impetuous subjects had acted without his knowledge. "If any other Partys of these Rebels" should visit Louisiana, Chester warned, he would take offense should Unzaga attempt to supply them or grant protection to any of their boats "which may pass up, or down the River Mississippi, by Claiming them as [Spanish] properties and under that pretence, prevent their being visited when they pass" British territory. Since Unzaga was relieved of his duties as governor of Louisiana shortly after receiving this communiqué, he never responded to Chester's threat of reprisals. His successor, Governor Bernardo de Gálvez, wisely permitted the matter to rest there. Although Chester decided not to press the issue, he later notified British officials that Gálvez was "not Explicit upon the Subject of Suffering the Rebels to be supplied in His Government, with Ammunition." [20]

Through the winter of 1776–77, Chester kept receiving fresh reports of a projected American invasion of West Florida. For example, William Tracey, who claimed to be a deserter from the American army, and Superintendent Stuart warned him that the rebels were assembling a force of several thousand men and several hundred canoes capable of carrying twelve to fifteen persons each at Long Island on the Holston River near the Virginia border. According to Stuart, who counted 300 canoes on the river, the Americans planned to attack Mobile and Pensacola in the spring by way of the Tennessee and Tombigbee rivers. The western settlers could not forget the ease with which Gibson had descended the Mississippi River and Linn had ascended it with military supplies, and these memories kept them on edge. Although Chester appeared sympathetic to their pleas for protection, he was too short-handed at Pensacola and Mobile to furnish them with any military assistance. [21]

Despite Chester's growing concern about the safety of the province, British officials in London dismissed him as an alarmist and tried to convince him that West Florida was in no immediate danger from an American invasion or from wholesale defection of southern Indians as he seemed to think. Germain discounted Chester's dire warnings of an impending disaster and assured the governor that the Choctaws were prepared "to watch over the navigation of the Mississippi" and to protect the western flank from foreign attack. Although not completely relieved by Germain's reassurances, Chester was grateful for what little assistance he received from London. When subsequent events failed to confirm his grim predictions, Chester himself became more complacent and began to treat later reports of rebel designs on West Florida with greater aplomb.[22]

With the coming of spring, Chester's spirits showed marked improvement. With each passing week, he became more convinced than before that the rumored invasion of West Florida would not materialize. News from the East was even better. The British under General William Howe had taken Long Island in New York, and General George Washington's Continental Army was on the run. Only Washington's surprise attack against the German mercenaries at Trenton on Christmas Eve of 1776 interrupted a string of British victories which extended into the summer months of 1777. Before the year was out, Chester fully expected the Americans to lay down their arms.

The departure of the American patriot George Gibson from New Orleans in the late fall of 1776 was the beginning and not the end of serious controversy between England and Spain. Gálvez's decision in the spring of 1777 to order the seizure of eleven boats owned by British merchants who resided in New Orleans for engaging in contraband trade signaled a new direction in Spanish policy.

Since 1763, when Louisiana had become a Spanish colony, officials in that province had usually tolerated violations of the trade laws, because the inhabitants were so dependent upon imports which only the English could supply in sufficient quantity. Furthermore, Indians in the Southwest had grown accustomed to English or French provisions, and they always disliked and in some cases refused to accept inferior Spanish goods. Once the English had settled Manchac, Baton Rouge, and Natchez during the early 1770s, this trade became so common that the settlers coined the term "going to Little Manchac" to describe the widespread smuggling which centered there. Consequently, a number of English merchants set up residence in New Orleans to take better advantage of these profitable enterprises.

Although Governor O'Reilly made some effort to stamp out this illicit trade, he was only partially successful. During Unzaga's lengthier administration, the amount of smuggling increased perceptibly, largely because the governor was only halfhearted in his attempts to prevent it. Even the British merchants acknowledged that they were "treated with the greatest indulgence" and that "every privilege we could wish for was on the slightest application granted to us." [23]

At first, Gálvez was as lenient on the smugglers as his predecessor had been. Abruptly and without any advance notice, however, he reversed himself in April of 1777 and inaugurated a determined effort to curtail, if not wipe out, all British commerce on the lower Mississippi River. Since first arriving in Louisiana, Gálvez had been anxious to suppress British smuggling and to promote, as recent instructions from Madrid required, increased commerce with France and her West Indian colonies. He also realized, however, that the inhabitants, who had come to rely on English goods, would never support his policies without good cause. Knowing that complete public confidence was essential if he were to eliminate British smuggling on the Mississippi, Gálvez patiently waited for the right moment. When it appeared, he acted with alacrity. The unexpected seizure by a British sloop of war of a Spanish schooner and two canoes on Lake Pontchartrain for allegedly engaging in illicit trade with West Florida presented Gálvez with the excuse he needed.[24]

On the night of April 17, 1777, Gálvez sent parties of Spanish soldiers up and down the Mississippi River with orders to seize every British vessel between Manchac and the Balize. Only two ships, a sea-bound brig the *Jesse* and another vessel "anchored very far in the Offing," escaped Gálvez's well-laid trap. In all the Spaniards grabbed eleven British vessels—six brigs, three sloops, and two schooners—containing cargoes whose value exceeded $50,000. The captured merchandise was deposited in public warehouses, and the crews were placed in confinement—officers in the guardhouse and sailors in the common jail. At subsequent public auctions, the ships and cargoes were sold for about $53,000. On April 18, Gálvez carried his new policy one step further by commanding all British merchants to leave the province within fifteen days and by prohibiting Spanish subjects from receiving "into their homes or habitations any stranger whatsoever." [25]

In defending his actions against British protests, Gálvez placed the entire blame upon Lieutenant George Burdon, who was responsible for seizing the Spanish vessels on Lake Pontchartrain. Governor Chester believed that the Spanish governor had acted out of spite. In his letters to Madrid, however, Gálvez made it clear that he used the activities of the British sloop *West Florida* as a convenient excuse for enforcing the king's orders to curtail smuggling. Gálvez boasted that he had delivered such a crippling blow to British traders on the Mississippi that they would "not think of returning to carry on their clandestine commerce" for some time. On the other hand, Chester feared that the decrees were merely part of a general plan to step up aid to the American rebels. Consequently, he felt compelled to register a vigorous protest.[26] The arrival in the Mississippi River of the *Atalanta*, a British frigate under the command of Captain Thomas Lloyd, shortly after Gálvez's confiscation of the eleven vessels was fortuitous for Governor Chester. As a result he was able to learn most of the details surrounding the affair quicker than he ordinarily would have. Although Captain Lloyd was ostensibly on his way to Manchac, he was actually on the lookout for American privateers. On April 21, he stopped two vessels several leagues south of New Orleans. After firing on the *Marie*, a Spanish boat, Lloyd ordered his men, armed "with pistols and sabres," to board the *Margarita* even though it was flying the French flag. Once Lloyd determined that neither was a rebel vessel, he permitted both to proceed unharmed.

Even before Captain Lloyd reached New Orleans, he learned of Gálvez's seizure of the eleven British-owned boats, and he immediately sent the governor a polite note of protest. In the exchange of letters which followed, the Spanish governor rebuked the English captain for stopping and searching vessels engaged in legitimate commerce, and Lloyd reminded Gálvez of England's right under the treaty of 1763 to navigate the Mississippi freely. While acknowledging that England possessed this right, Gálvez asserted that it did not extend to contraband trade nor did it permit the British to moor their ships on Spanish territory.

Although Gálvez adopted a hard line and later boasted that he had received the British "with match in hand," he was obviously relieved when, on May 12, the *Atalanta* unexpectedly dropped sail and headed south to investigate rumors of an American privateer at the mouth of the Mississippi River. Apparently the reports were true, because Gálvez informed Lloyd that the Spanish king had granted immunity to all

American ships on the Mississippi and warned him that "whoever fights on the river will incur the disapproval of my sovereign." Captain Lloyd knew of the indulgences Gálvez had granted the American frigate *Columbus,* but he refrained from attacking her on his return to Pensacola.

Although Gálvez concluded that his bluff had worked, the English merchants of New Orleans—not the Spanish governor—were primarily responsible for Lloyd's decision to withdraw. In a letter dated April 26, five prominent British merchants refused to accept Lloyd's invitation to meet with him aboard the *Atalanta* or to give him details of the confiscations. Instead they praised the Spanish governor for the past courtesies he had shown them and urged Lloyd not to offend Gálvez, since he had "consented to our staying with the usual privileges for the collection of our debts and settlement of our affairs." They further pointed out to Lloyd that the Spanish governor held the power "to hurt the British merchants here far beyond the value of the Shipping seized." [27]

Rather than personally incurring responsibility for permanently jeopardizing British commerce on the lower Mississippi, Captain Lloyd preferred to place the matter in the hands of Governor Chester. After collecting as much information on the affair as he could from willing informers, Captain Lloyd arrived in Pensacola in early June and conferred at length with Chester. Acting upon the governor's recommendation, the Council of West Florida eventually decided to send two of its members—Lieutenant Colonel Alexander Dickson and John Stephenson, a prominent local merchant—to New Orleans where they were to meet with Governor Gálvez and demand the "immediate Restitution of all such Vessels, Cargoes, Goods, and Merchandise and other properties." If Gálvez refused to comply with their request, they were then to "obtain Affidavits relative to the seizures." Finally Dickson and Stephenson were to "inquire into the Countenance given Gibson last summer." [28]

The two British commissioners arrived in New Orleans in late July, but the discussions with Gálvez got off to a bad start. Incensed by Chester's instructions to the two Englishmen that they take depositions from Spanish subjects in order to determine if the seizures were legal, Gálvez sternly warned them that he would tolerate no such activity "even as far as my own House." To prove his contention that the seized vessels were engaged in illicit trade, the Spanish governor informed Dickson and Stephenson that several English prisoners had admitted their guilt in signed statements. The two Englishmen scoffed at the confessions, which they insisted were extracted under duress. "Fear on one side and hope on the other," they sneered, "concurred perhaps to their asserting Falsehoods." [29]

Unable to win their point that Spain had no right to stop British ships on the Mississippi River, Dickson and Stephenson moved to the attack. They accused Oliver Pollock, with Spanish connivance, of first outfitting an American privateer in New Orleans and then encouraging the crew to steal the cattle of Englishmen residing in Louisiana. Gálvez professed complete ignorance of these matters. He knew Pollock "in no other character than an honest Merchant, a Native of Ireland," and he was surprised "to learn that the Vessel was a Privateer" since he had thought it was registered under the name of an Englishman.

The only concession wrung from Gálvez was an admission that at least one of the eleven vessels seized was carrying not contraband but only Negroes and indigo. While he lamented the necessity of depriving a person who was unconnected with illicit trade of his property, Gálvez explained that it was impossible to catch the smugglers without seizing all British ships at the same time. "It was," the governor stated, "what may be called an unlucky moment" for the innocent party. In order to prove that his actions did not constitute a vendetta against the British, Gálvez reminded Dickson and Stephenson that two of the eleven vessels were owned by Americans. Of course, he did not tell them of his plans to compensate the Americans for their losses.[30]

After nearly a month of fruitless wrangling, the two commissioners finally gave in to Captain Lloyd's repeated importunities to leave New Orleans. The crew of the *Atalanta* was overcome with sickness, and the captain feared wholesale desertion, especially after he learned of Spanish efforts to encourage it. To keep desertion from reaching epidemic proportions, Lloyd ordered one of his officers to enter the home of a Spanish citizen after dark in pursuit of a deserter who had taken refuge there.[31] As all three British officials realized, successful negotiations were impossible under these conditions.

The return voyage was unexpectedly hazardous as prevailing winds swept the *Atalanta* off course and delayed her arrival in Pensacola until late September. After waiting anxiously for several weeks for the safe return of Dickson and Stephenson, Chester found their report disappointing. Not only had they failed to gain restoration of British property, but they also brought the disquieting news that the Americans were planning to send a "strong detachment against British posts in the Illinois Country" and then to "Erect a Fort near the mouth of the Ohio" River. Once these objectives were accomplished, the two commissioners reported, the Americans intended to establish regular trade up and down the Mississippi. Dickson and Stephenson also learned that Pollock, with Spanish approval, had contracted for the construction of "Six Gondolas or Row Galleys" of eighty to a hundred oars each to convey arms and ammunition up the river. They also learned that "two of the Galleys are already begun upon."

Although not fully appreciated at the time, one additional piece of intelligence proved particularly distressing, because it threatened to place British commerce on the Mississippi at a permanent disadvantage. Through a series of proclamations, beginning in early 1777 and extending through the summer, Gálvez granted enlarged privileges to French merchants. The Spanish governor readily acknowledged to all interested parties his intention of making New Orleans a free port, while continuing to deny British merchants access to the city's wharves. By late spring, two French commissioners were in New Orleans to promote their nation's commercial interests. By midsummer, the once brisk British trade on the lower Mississippi was all but eliminated. "The British flag has not appeared on this river for more than three months," the French commissioners wrote on July 18, and "the whole trade of the Mississippi is now in our hands." [32]

While British commerce on the Mississippi decreased noticeably during the latter half of 1777, American traffic, much of it disguised as Spanish trade, increased several fold, due largely to the enterprise of Pollock and the collusion of Gálvez. Before the year ended, Pollock, assisted by Spanish loans in excess of $70,000, had dispatched several shiploads of provisions and military equipment up the Mississippi to posts along the Ohio River in the states of Pennsylvania and Virginia. In early 1778, Pollock arranged for shipment of a wide assortment of merchandise, valued at 10,000 pistoles and consigned to the Commerce Committee of the Continental Congress. Designed for the comfort as well as the protection of American frontiersmen fighting to protect the western settlements, this cargo included not only the usual amount of powder, gunlocks, and musketballs, but also such items as ivory combs, handkerchiefs, needles, tablecloths, men's hats and shoes, fine ruffled shirts, red garters, wine, brandy, and taffia, as well as "a box of Havanna Segars" for Pollock's friend Robert Morris.

To finance the loans required for payment of these articles, Pollock was forced to mortgage a large part of his personal property, including land and slaves. He hoped to repay Spain for her advances by purchasing indigo and peltries at cheap western prices and reselling them to the French at a quick profit. In addition, he expected to secure revenue from the sale of prizes brought to New Orleans by American privateers. To assist Pollock in these commercial endeavors, Gálvez permitted American ships to be treated as Spanish property in order to protect them from the vigilance of British cruisers. With the governor's consent, Pollock specifically instructed the captains of vessels carrying American goods upstream as well as those descending the river to call only at Spanish posts along the way and to be on the lookout for hostile Indians and British troops. Although supplies sent from New Orleans were never large enough to be decisive in the war effort, they were still of some aid to the American cause.[33]

By late 1777, Governor Chester had come to discount the likelihood of an American invasion in the foreseeable future, but members of the Council of West Florida were not so sanguine and English settlers along the Mississippi lived in constant fear of a "Rebel attack or a rupture with Spain." Each fresh rumor of impending danger circulated freely between Manchac and Natchez, and hardly a month passed without at least one report of a planned American incursion or a Spanish declaration of war. By early 1778, even the settlers along the

Mississippi were becoming immune to these scares and less certain the war would penetrate their corner of the world.[34]

At the end of 1777, the uneasy peace which had characterized relations between England and Spain in the Gulf region since early 1776 remained unchanged. This situation was due more to international conditions than to developments in the Southwest. The British still hoped to restrict the war to a family quarrel and to avoid another general European conflict. Spain was not yet ready to embrace the cause of revolution or to cooperate fully with her old Bourbon ally in Europe by joining France in supporting the American rebels in the faint hope of weakening Great Britain. For the most part, British and Spanish officials at home either urged caution on the part of colonial officers or refrained from providing them with the means to wage war. Although Governor Gálvez was more willing to support the American cause than most of his superiors in Madrid and Havana, he too was careful to conceal his activities lest he later be accused of provoking the British into retaliatory action. In the final analysis, decisions made in London and Madrid and not those actions taken in New Orleans and Pensacola were primarily responsible for maintaining the fragile truce in the Southwest.

3

An American Raider

IF officials in Spanish Louisiana and British West Florida were determined to maintain peace in the Southwest, the same was not true of a number of Americans who had commercial ties in the lower Mississippi Valley and who entertained hopes of establishing regular trade between the Ohio settlements and New Orleans. Foremost among these individuals was George Morgan whose interest in the Southwest extended as far back as 1766 when he had first visited Natchez.

In 1776, Morgan, holding the military rank of colonel, was at Fort Pitt serving the United States as agent for Indian affairs and as deputy commissary general of purchase in the Western District. Charged with the responsibility of converting Fort Pitt into an important depot of military supplies for use against the Indians, Colonel Morgan knew the advantages of opening up a brisk trade along the Mississippi with the Spaniards in Louisiana. In fact, he was not only at Fort Pitt when Lieutenant Linn arrived in the spring of 1777 with the first shipment of powder from New Orleans, but he was also fully aware of Gibson's purposes in going south.

Morgan seized the opportunity afforded by Gibson's return to initiate a lively correspondence with Governor Gálvez in hopes of obtaining additional supplies and of securing Spanish permission to launch an American attack on British forts in

West Florida. In his first letter of April 22, 1777, Morgan agreed to "pay liberally to have a plan of the fortifications [at Mobile and Pensacola], and correct information as to the garrisons and naval forces which protect these places." The colonel also asked Gálvez if he thought "one thousand men were sufficient for the contemplated expedition" and if the American invaders "could, in New Orleans, purchase or charter vessels, at a short notice and procure cannon." Of course, Morgan assured the Spanish governor, "we shall never proceed to any action on the subject" without first obtaining "the permission and co-operation of your Excellency." [1]

Gálvez's reply of August 9 was cordial but circumspect. He assured Morgan of his desire to aid the American cause, but he also informed him that he could not officially permit "the hiring or purchasing" of vessels in New Orleans. Even though he personally could not take part in such transactions, Gálvez hinted that he would not object if Morgan undertook "an agreement with the same person" who had earlier supplied Gibson with provisions. "You may be assured," Gálvez declared, "that I shall lend my permission and all the aid I can, not withstanding that I shall apparently feign not to understand anything about the matter." [2]

Morgan's candid overtures to Gálvez were but a small part of an overall plan to promote an American attack on British West Florida. Morgan had also been discussing with a number of eastern business associates and a handful of his personal acquaintances in the Continental Congress the feasibility of sending an armed expedition down the Ohio and Mississippi rivers comparable in size to the one which had unsuccessfully invaded Canada during the winter of 1775–76. By late 1776, a majority of Congress favored a plan which would permit Spain to capture Pensacola and to possess it permanently if she agreed to declare war against Great Britain and allowed the United States free navigation of the Mississippi River and full use of the harbor at Pensacola. Even after these efforts came to nothing, Morgan continued to promote the scheme among his congressional friends.

In early June, Congress asked Benedict Arnold, one of the American generals involved in the ill-fated Canadian venture, for an opinion on the subject. Ironically, Arnold turned to Morgan, one of the few easterners with any firsthand knowledge of Pensacola, for advice in writing up a report which he eventually submitted to the Board of War in early July. In a seven-page memorandum, Morgan described in minute detail conditions as he knew them in the Southwest. He recommended sending a force of 1,500 men with enough supplies to reach New Orleans, where they could obtain from the Spaniards additional powder and provisions for an attack on Pensacola and possibly on Mobile as well. In case the raiders were successful in seizing the two Gulf ports, Morgan favored retaining the towns rather than ceding them to Spain as Gibson had earlier proposed to Governor Unzaga.[3]

On July 11, 1777, the Board of War accepted the Arnold report which was actually based on Morgan's suggestions. The board recommended that "an expedition be undertaken against Pensacola and Mobile [and] . . . that Colonel George Morgan be sent to New Orleans with power to negotiate with the governor of that place." In the board's opinion, a force of 1,000 men under the command of General Edward Hand, commander of Fort Pitt, should be sent down the Mississippi as soon as possible.[4]

Congress debated the report for two days. The principal spokesman in support of the board's recommendation was Robert Morris of Pennsylvania. Not only was Morris a friend of Morgan, but he was also a business partner of Oliver Pollock with whom he had kept in close touch. Relying on information received from Pollock and other western informants, Morris assured Congress that the British had no more than 300 soldiers to defend the Mississippi frontier and that the small cost of the proposed expedition would be more than offset by the proceeds from seizure of English provisions and military stores. In addition, the expedition could result in important commercial trade advantages for the United States, since it might remove all obstacles to a permanent trade between Spanish New Orleans and the upper Ohio Valley.

To guarantee the attainment of these objectives, Morris impressed upon Congress the necessity of quick action since delay might permanently jeopardize the operation. Another Pennsylvanian, James Wilson, spoke in favor of sending an expedition down the Mississippi River, but he opposed attacking Mobile and Pensacola because of the greater risk attending that part of the project. In contrast to Morris, who underscored the advantages to be gained from the assault, Wilson concentrated upon the absence of risk involved in his more limited plan since the Mississippi River afforded the invaders with a safe path of retreat. He agreed with Morris that considerable damage could be inflicted upon English settlements along the Mississippi. Benjamin Harrison, a Virginian and friend of Governor Patrick Henry whose interest in Spanish trade was well known, vigorously supported the entire Board of War's recommendations. Harrison argued that the attack would weaken British influence among the southern Indians, provide the United States with much needed supplies, and strengthen American ties with Spanish Louisiana.[5]

Strongest opposition to the project came from delegates of the lower South. As one of these opponents of the invasion,

Arthur Middleton of South Carolina argued that such an enterprise might "draw the attention of the enemy to the southern states." The most effective critic was another South Carolinian, Henry Laurens, who had taken his seat in Congress only two days before debate on the board's report commenced. According to him, support for the proposal was so strong when he arrived in Philadelphia that "nothing remained to do . . . but vote Men and Money." Agreeing completely with Middleton's assessment of the dangers involved, Laurens launched a vigorous counterattack by raising a number of embarrassing questions. If Congress had a thousand troops to spare, Laurens asked, would it not be better to use them in defending Georgia and South Carolina?

Laurens also wondered if a thousand men were enough to dislodge the British from West Florida when they were constantly being reinforced by a steady influx of displaced Loyalists from the eastern part of the United States. Finally, Laurens asserted, it was folly to imagine, as supporters of the proposal apparently did, that the British would not learn of the expedition before it reached the lower Mississippi. In the face of Laurens' probing analysis, support for the project quickly evaporated, and Congress agreed on July 25 to postpone further consideration of the Mississippi expedition. "I delivered my sentiments and was successful," Laurens boasted to a friend; "the question had scarcely an affirmative." [6]

Morris was not one to give up easily, however. Thwarted in his earlier efforts to gain immediate congressional sanction but convinced that the time was ripe for a southwestern adventure, he persuaded his colleagues on the Committee of Commerce (formerly known as the Secret Committee) to support a smaller and less expensive expedition with a more limited objective. This committee, as its former name implied, operated less openly than the full Congress and functioned as a sort of executive department during much of the war. Laurens, as the newly elected president of the Congress, was a member of this important committee, but Morris eventually won him over to his way of thinking. At least Laurens raised no serious objections to a scaled-down version of the earlier plans and acquiesced when the committee agreed to send a small party of men to New Orleans from Fort Pitt without seeking approval of the full Congress.[7]

During the period when these plans were being secretly discussed in committee, James Willing, younger brother of Morris's business partner, Thomas Willing, suddenly appeared in York, Pennsylvania, where the government had temporarily taken refuge after the British seized Philadelphia. Young Willing was probably there at the insistence of Oliver Pollock, who was even more anxious than Morris for an expedition against British West Florida.[8]

From the viewpoints of Morris and Pollock, James Willing was the perfect person to lead a small party of Americans down the Mississippi. Not only were his close connections with prominent eastern merchants much to their liking, but, more importantly, he was thoroughly familiar with the situation in the Southwest, having resided there for at least four years prior to his return to the East in the fall of 1777. James Willing, whose older brother was a senior partner in the influential Philadelphia firm of Willing & Morris and a member of the First Continental Congress, had moved to Natchez in the summer of 1772, expecting in a short period of time to become a leading planter and merchant.

As a first step in obtaining his goals, James Willing went to Pensacola where he secured from the Council of West Florida 1,250 acres of land along the eastern bank of the Mississippi, most of it located just north of Baton Rouge. He then proceeded to New Orleans where he contacted Oliver Pollock, who agreed to assist him in securing "a contract to supply the [British] Troops at Pensacola with Flour etc." Since Pollock had earlier obtained a similar arrangement with the Spanish, the two of them were in a position to guarantee delivery of almost any product needed by the British, "particular[ly] as the whole comes through the channel of Messrs. Willing and Morris." General Frederick Haldimand, commanding officer of British forces in West Florida, was unimpressed with the proposal, and Willing was never able to secure the lucrative contract he sought. Frustrated by these failures and unfamiliar with agricultural pursuits, Willing allowed numerous opportunities for financial gain to escape his grasp. He came increasingly to devote more time to pleasure than to business and soon squandered his small fortune in drink and other forms of riotous living. With the outbreak of the American Revolution in 1775, Willing quickly made himself unpopular with a number of inhabitants by his frequent and boisterous declarations in behalf of the American cause. By early 1777, there was nothing to keep him in the Southwest, and he left Natchez deeply embittered by these unpleasant experiences.[9]

Once in Pennsylvania, Willing discussed conditions in the Southwest with several former acquaintances and a few selected members of Congress. Although he painted a rosier picture of the situation there than the facts warranted, he confirmed the impressions of Morgan and Morris that the region was daily growing more Tory in sentiment. On the other hand, Willing assured his eager listeners that the more substantial inhabitants were either pro-American or uncommitted and that they would flock to the patriot standard if protected by American troops. At any rate, he promised that he could secure the neutrality if not the support of most inhabitants in the western part of West Florida.[10]

By late November, 1777, a majority on the Commerce Committee agreed to send James Willing and a small number of soldiers on a secret mission down the Ohio and Mississippi rivers to New Orleans. Acting in its capacity as commercial agent of the government, the committee decided not to seek the approval of Congress. In a carefully worded message, two members of the committee—Morris and William Smith of Maryland—instructed General Edward Hand, commanding officer at Fort Pitt, to outfit Willing with a "Continental [boat] properly manned, armed, and provisioned to carry him . . . to New Orleans." Although the committee left the number of men, the amount of arms, and the quantity of provisions "to Hand's discretion," Willing later stated that he was authorized to recruit twenty-four men. The ostensible purpose of Willing's expedition was to convey some "P[ublic] dispatches" to officials in Louisiana, and the committee was content to let the rest of Congress believe that was the only objective.[11]

Armed with the Commerce Committee's letter to General Hand, a letter to Oliver Pollock in New Orleans, and a commission for himself as captain in the United States Navy, Willing arrived at Fort Pitt in mid-December. Although General Hand was away at the time, he acted upon his return with dispatch in outfitting Willing's small force despite his own misgivings about the timing of the expedition. "I . . . am afraid the river will be shut up before he gets away," Hand lamented. Colonel Morgan shared Hand's opinion, believing that if the expedition was to have any chance of success it would have to depart from Fort Pitt no later than the first of October. "You should now be about leaving New Orleans to ascend the river," Morgan wrote Willing, and "thereby secure your passage at one third of the Expence . . . . I now dread the Issue." [12]

By Christmas Day, Willing had been equipped with an armed boat named the U.S.S. *Rattletrap* and with a "volunteer crew" of one captain, two sergeants, and twenty-six privates. In addition Willing persuaded Ensign Thomas McIntire, who had just been released from a British prison camp, to accompany him to New Orleans "in the character of his Lieutenant." The departure from Fort Pitt, however, was delayed for another two weeks while Willing worked out arrangements for obtaining the necessary supplies both for his journey down the Mississippi as well as for his return upstream. Since he "expect[ed] to bring at least five Boats from New Orleans laden with dry goods and navigated by 20 or 25 men each," he requested a "sufficient quantity" of provisions "to be lodged for me by the beginning of April next at the Arkansaws." In early January, Colonel Morgan issued him enough flour, pork, and beef to sustain "30 men [for] 180 Days," although the "70 Galls. Of Whiskey" he received, if rationed out at the ratio of "½ pint pr man pr day, [would] last 30 days" only.[13]

At last, on January 11, 1778, the *Rattletrap* and its crew, commanded by James Willing (who was to sign his official correspondence "Captn. In the Service of the Indept. United States of America"), began their descent of the Ohio River, picking up additional recruits as they proceeded. Shortly thereafter, rumors began to circulate throughout the Illinois country concerning their immediate destination. The French commander of the English post at Kaskaskia, Philippe de Rocheblave, who maintained a handful of spies on the Mississippi, believed the party was headed for the upper Illinois territory. After learning that Willing had seized two brothers and their peltries as well as a Frenchman and his cargo of brandy on his way down the Ohio, Rocheblave braced for an attack. Willing would have liked nothing better than to teach the "damned Rogues" of Kaskaskia, including "their ancient Leader Rocheblave," a lesson or two, but he had orders to head south rather than north when he came to the Mississippi River. Somewhere between the falls of the Ohio and Fort Pitt, Willing intercepted a letter to George Morgan from Francisco Cruzat, lieutenant governor of Spanish Illinois who was stationed at St. Louis, and put his endorsement on it. "Recd and Examined this 17 Jany 1778, J. Willing," he hurriedly noted.[14]

Word of a possible attack on West Florida reached British Indian agents in the upper Mississippi in early February. Another Frenchman, this one an American deserter, reported that the rebels had amassed a sizable flotilla on the upper Ohio, but the British treated this intelligence with no more concern than they had the numerous other rumors which made their way into West Florida. Indeed, British officials had good reason to disregard this one since even the informer admitted that the Americans had delayed too long and were frozen in.[15]

Although John Stuart had repeatedly urged British Indian agents in the Choctaw nation to maintain a close watch of the Mississippi River and although Governor Chester had assured Lord Germain that the Choctaws were prepared to attack any vessel which attempted to descend the river, this well-conceived surveillance nonetheless broke down in early February, just a few weeks before Willing reached the Arkansas River. Since General Hand planned to store supplies at the Spanish post there for use of the Americans when they returned north, Willing was anxious to clear the area of all potential enemies. Consequently, after his men had plundered the property of the small settlement of English and French

fur traders who resided on the English side at Concord, Willing ordered the place abandoned.

At least one victim of Willing's raid at Concord, an impover-
ished trader named Michael Hooppack, joined Willing's party,
presumably in hopes of recovering his property from Spanish
officials in New Orleans. There may have been others who
enlisted in the invading ranks, for by the time Willing reached
the mouth of the Yazoo River his original force of thirty men
had grown to nearly a hundred. Whether by design or by
accident, fourteen Americans arrived at Concord a few days
after Willing left and petitioned Governor Gálvez to "take
them under your Protection," on the excuse that since the
English side of the river was deserted they were afraid of an
Indian attack.[16]

From Concord, Willing's "Body of Banditti," which now
purportedly amounted "in the whole to about one hundred
Men," proceeded south to Walnut Hills where Colonel Stuart
had stationed a handful of Indian agents and a party of Choctaws "as a guard for protection of the river." Unknown to
Willing, the Indians had returned to their nation a few weeks
earlier. Although the British agents had tried to prevent them
from leaving, they were not terribly disappointed when the
Choctaws departed because, as one of them explained, "as for
one batteau coming down, I do not think they will venture
as they cannot but hear we are lying in wait for them." Furthermore, winter seemed the most unlikely time for the
Americans to launch an invasion. Despite the reasonableness
of these assumptions, they proved extremely costly to the exposed British settlers along the Mississippi and unbelievably
fortunate for Willing and his band of intrepid adventurers.[17]

While a second party of some fifty Choctaws was on the way
to Walnut Hills to replace the recently departed detachment,

an advance contingent of approximately forty Americans under the command of Lieutenant McIntire arrived in two small
barges during the brief interval between shifts. At ten o'clock
on the night of February 18, the Americans came ashore and
surprised four unsuspecting British Indian agents who were
enjoying themselves at the home of John Watkins. The Americans remained only long enough to ascertain the identity of
their five captives and to seize a few of Watkins's weapons.
When Watkins assured McIntire's troops that he was not in
British pay, they released him after he took an oath of neutrality. Two hours later, they departed Walnut Hills, accompanied by the four Indian agents who were their prisoners.

At daybreak the next morning, Willing and the rest of his
force, numbering about sixty men, arrived at Watkins's plantation. A small detachment of five men came ashore and informed Watkins that "they were going to New Orleans, where
they intended to try their prisoners and dispose of their plunder." Furthermore, they threatened to "put to death without
reserve" all deserters from their ranks and "all persons whom
they should take employed in the Indian department." The
next day, John Watkins set out for Pensacola to alert British
officials.[18]

While drifting down the Mississippi on the way to the next
scheduled stop at Natchez, McIntire's small flotilla captured
a small batteau anchored near the shore a few yards north of
Cole's Creek. The batteau contained three Natchez settlers
—Alexander McIntosh, William Eason, and William Williams—who were going to the Spanish post on the Arkansas
River. When the three men identified themselves, McIntire
recognized the name of McIntosh as a person on Willing's
extensive blacklist. He immediately informed the three Englishmen that they were prisoners of war and sardonically told

McIntosh, "We will take care of you [because] that damned scoundrel James Willing is come once more to pay You a visit." McIntosh interpreted that comment as a none too subtle reference to a "former Expression about Willing" he had made. The American lieutenant placed the three Englishmen on board his barge while his men steered their batteau downstream. Before this party reached Natchez, another large batteau commanded by Robert George, nephew of George Rogers Clark, joined the McIntire party and together they continued the journey downstream.[19]

The rebels hurried to Natchez, their first important destination. Judging from the actions his men took there, Willing had two primary objectives in mind. Foremost was a desire to settle old scores with a handful of former acquaintances whom he had come to despise while a resident of West Florida. At the top of his blacklist was former British army officer Anthony Hutchins, an outspoken Tory magistrate of the Natchez District and squire of White Apple Village. Not far below Hutchins's name was that of Alexander McIntosh, another prominent planter with strong British leanings. To make certain that the property of neither of these two gentlemen escaped his net, Willing ordered McIntire's advance squadron to slip past Natchez under the cover of darkness and to proceed immediately to Hutchins's and McIntosh's plantations and seize their slaves.[20]

McIntire split his party into pairs—one faction headed for McIntosh's home, knowing that the master was absent, while the other went straight to Hutchins's plantation in hopes of surprising him and his family. After killing several of McIntosh's cattle and a few of his hogs, the Americans ransacked his house and took "about half a dozen of his negroes" to the Natchez landing. Meanwhile, Lieutenant McIntire and the larger of the two parties pulled Hutchins out of his sickbed and forced him and "three or four of his slaves" to accompany them to White Cliffs, about fifteen miles south of Natchez, where the Americans had hidden two barges. There they placed the Negroes on "Capt. [Thomas] Barber's flat laden with corn" while Hutchins was "taken as a prisoner aboard said M'Intire's boat." The next day, Willing himself paid the Hutchins family a personal visit, and Anthony's son John had no trouble recalling the incident years later. "He demanded of my mother her gold and silver," John Hutchins remembered, "and such other articles as he might wish to place his hands on." When Mrs. Hutchins made no move to comply with his instructions, Willing "lifted from his belt a pistol and pointed it at her breast." Undaunted, she retorted, "Shoot coward, I am but a woman." Temporarily shaken by this display of courage, Willing put his pistol back in his belt and, "seeing a large chest in one of the corners of the house[,] threw open the lid and running his hand to the bottom he got hold of a leather bag of bullets." Believing that it contained specie, Willing ordered his men to stop searching the house and to round up the rest of Hutchins's slaves. Leaving only a Negro woman in childbirth behind, the Americans headed back to Natchez. [21]

While these events were taking place south of the settlement, the main body of Willing's men landed at Natchez on the evening of February 19. Early the following morning, Willing hoisted the American flag over Fort Panmure and "sent out sundry parties" into the countryside informing the inhabitants that they were prisoners of the United States "on parole" and ordering them to appear before the captain as soon as possible. All who refused to obey voluntarily were forcibly brought before Willing. When settler Donald McPherson ignored their orders, some of Willing's men bound his hands and dragged him into town. To encourage compliance with their orders, Willing's men exaggerated the size of their own force and frightened many of the settlers into believing that Colonel Morgan was on his way to Natchez with 2,000 men.[22]

Fearful of the wholesale confiscation of their property and of their own imprisonment, the residents of Natchez "thought it necessary to go to the said Willing to propose measures" of accommodation. Consequently, they "unanimously delegated" William Hiorn, Charles Percy, Samuel Wells, and Lucas Collins "to treat in their name for a capitulation, which should be formed in the best terms possible." In turn, the four planters asked Isaac Johnson, Richard Ellis, and Joseph Thompson to join them as "associates" in conducting negotiations with the Americans.

In an agreement signed with Willing on February 21, the citizens of Natchez pledged to "not in any wise take up arms against the United States of America or aid, abet or in any wise give assistance to the enemies" of that government. In return, Captain Willing promised that, as long as the settlers remained neutral, he would respect their "persons, slaves and other property of whatever description" and "that he would send a flag of truce to the Choctaw Nation . . . to prevent the Indians [from] falling on this Defenceless District."

Willing had originally planned to execute Robert Welsh, because the latter had been carrying at the time of his capture an order from Farquhar Bethune, British commissary for the Choctaw nation, "to obstruct, harrass, distress, and oppose any party of Americans coming down the river." However, the captain agreed to send Welsh "with a flag to the Choctaws since he had great influence with that tribe." For their part, the Natchez delegates consented to send a copy of these arti-

cles to Governor Chester along with a request that he likewise
urge the Indians not to molest the inhabitants of Natchez.
Finally, the delegates took a prescribed oath of neutrality "on
behalf of the people" and designated William Hiorn to accompany Willing and his men to New Orleans as surety for their
part of the bargain.[23]

In addition to plundering the property of a few notorious
Loyalists and neutralizing the rest of the settlement, Willing
managed to attract several new recruits to his ranks during
his five-day stay in the Natchez area. He scored his greatest
success among those settlers "well disposed to the American
cause." Armed with blank commissions, he recruited a handful of subordinates, including James "flat-nosed" Eliot and the
Harrison brothers, Robert and Reuben. As a "man of in-
genuity and address," Willing pleaded "the cause of America
with persuasive eloquence." By emphasizing "the justness of
their warfare, the bravery of their soldiers, and the moral
certainty of their ultimate success," he won over almost a
hundred new adherents. According to a dismayed John Fitzpatrick, a number of these men were his debtors, which may
have accounted for their desire to leave the district with
Willing.[24]

Meanwhile, as negotiations continued at Natchez, McIntire
and fifteen of his men left for New Orleans with Anthony
Hutchins, all his slaves, and most of his movable property.
Because of torrential spring rains, the Mississippi River was
extremely high and swift, allowing McIntire and his party to
pass down the river so rapidly that inhabitants along the way
were unable to detect them. The group reached the southernmost English settlement of Manchac even before their friends
in New Orleans had expected. Early on the morning of February 23, McIntire and his men, aided by a dense fog, surprised

and captured the British ship *Rebecca* "late of London, John Cox master, mounted with sixteen carriage guns, 4 pounders, besides Swivels." Before proceeding to New Orleans as originally planned, they waited at Manchac for the main body of Willing's force, which arrived a few days later augmented by "3 or 4 people of the Natchez settlement, a number of French and Spanish batteau men, Hunters & other Banditti." [25] With the addition of these last reinforcements, the number of men in Willing's party now totaled nearly 200.

As Willing drew closer to the site of his earlier residence just north of Baton Rouge, he became bolder and acted with less leniency toward his former neighbors. Between British Pointe Coupée and Manchac, Willing's raiders pillaged several plantations (looting some and burning others to the ground), seized scores of helpless and frightened black slaves, and wantonly destroyed livestock of every description. As they had done in Natchez, the Americans were again selective in their choice of victims. At Baton Rouge, they seized only half the property on George Castles' plantation because they considered his partner a patriot and left the property of two other nearby planters completely unmolested.

Surprisingly, the settlers at Pointe Coupée and Baton Rouge were no better prepared for Willing's appearance than those at Natchez had been. The first news received by these inhabitants of American invaders in the vicinity came from Manchac when they learned of McIntire's seizure of the *Rebecca*. By the time William Dunbar arrived in Manchac to investigate this report, McIntire and his men already "had dropped down below the Town to be more safe," and he foolishly thought the crisis was over. Although Dunbar prudently moved his slaves to "the Spanish side" of the river, he failed to take any further precautions, and when he departed for Pointe Coupée he left all his other property behind except what was necessary for the voyage.

Upon arriving at his destination, Dunbar was shocked when he ran into a panic-stricken Harry Alexander just after he had escaped "with his negroes . . . from the English side." Alexander told him that James Willing was on the river at the head of a raiding party and that the Americans intended "to rob & plunder every English subject who had property of any value" except for a favored few. "Several obnoxious people" including himself and Dunbar, Alexander had learned, "were to meet with particular marks of their displeasure." Dunbar's initial reaction was one of disbelief. He found it difficult to understand why Willing wanted to plunder the property of men in "whose houses he had been often entertained in the most hospitable manner" and who had in the past "frequently indulged his natural propensity of getting Drunk." [27]

But Willing soon made a believer out of Dunbar and almost every other settler along the eastern bank of the Mississippi from Natchez to Manchac. Planters in and around Baton Rouge sustained heavy losses, as the devastation wrought by Willing's men was almost complete. "They have cleared all the English side of the river of inhabitants," wrote one observer, and there was "nothing to be seen but Destruction and Desolation." Miraculously no one was killed, although there were a few narrow escapes. The superintendent's younger brother, Henry Stuart—another person on Willing's lengthy blacklist —was "obliged to fly in his shirt to the Spanish Fort at Manchac" barely ahead of his pursuers who tried unsuccessfully to bribe the corporal of the fort into turning him over to them. Rumor had it that the Americans planned to slice Harry Alexander "into hundred pieces" and to flay Alexander Ross alive when they captured them, but fortunately both men also stayed a step ahead of their pursuers.[28]

Dunbar returned to his plantation in time to watch in disgust as Willing's "Troop of Rascalls" ransacked his own home and those of his neighbors to the north and the south of him. They spared nothing. "All was fish that came into their nett," Dunbar wrote. It took the raiders three or four trips to strip Dunbar of all his personal property, but eventually they carted off everything in sight. "All my waring apparell, bed & table linen," he recalled in his diary; "not a shirt was left in the house—blankets, pieces of cloth, sugar, silver ware." In one sense, the Americans were well behaved. Instead of partaking of his liquor on the spot or carrying it off for later consumption, they "destroyed a considerable quantity of bottled wine." In all, Dunbar "was plundered of 1,200 [pounds] sterg. value."

On another occasion, Dunbar and his friends heard more than a hundred shots fired in the space of thirty minutes. Upon rushing over to investigate, the settlers discovered a number of Americans "employed in wantonly killing the Hogs & other stock upon the plantation." "The Houses were immediately rummaged & every thing of any value secured for the Comodore's use," Dunbar wrote; "after which the Heroick Captain ordered his people to set fire to all the houses & indigo works, which was accordingly done & they were quickly consumed to ashes." [29]

If the settlements of Pointe Coupée and Baton Rouge suffered severely from the plundering, Manchac was not overlooked. John Fitzpatrick alone sustained losses in excess of $13,000 and was forced for several months to transfer his commercial operations to "Spanish Manchac." At first, the town's

close proximity to Spanish territory proved advantageous
since the inhabitants could easily slip across the border with
their property. Later, as the Americans grew more and more
greedy, the region between Manchac and the Amite River
became a convenient target for additional pillage, as small
parties of Americans repeatedly visited the area and wreaked
havoc on the hapless settlers. In early April, while Dunbar was
going down the Mississippi to New Orleans, he passed "two
of the American boats on their way up again for more plunder." He later learned that these particular raiders went as far
north as Baton Rouge where they "surprised Messrs. Williams, Watts and Dicas [and] made them prisoners with all
their Negroes" even though all three had taken oaths of
neutrality." [30]

The extent and nature of depredations committed by Willing and his men against British settlers in West Florida instantly became a matter of controversy and has remained so
ever since. According to the British, the American raiders
were "no better than a group of outlaws and robbers," and
therefore beyond the protection of law. None of the Americans was even captured, but it was by no means certain that
the British would have treated them as prisoners of war. Although a handful of these men may have at one time or another
during the expedition worn military uniforms, the vast majority were dressed in the style of hunters and were armed with
a rifle, cutlass, and one or two pistols.[31]

On the other hand, Willing insisted that he was a captain
in the United States Navy. He treated the men as if they were
soldiers of the United States and granted officers' commissions
to several of his assistants. The Continental Congress later
approved these actions when it promoted two of the lieutenants to the rank of captain in recognition of their meritorious

service during Willing's expedition down the Mississippi River. While the original group of thirty men were unquestionably military personnel, the character of the later recruits ranged all the way from dedicated patriots to "Villians" and "free booters." [32]

Even more controversial was the question of whether Willing violated the terms of his agreement with British settlers, signed at Natchez on February 21, when he later ravaged the towns of Pointe Coupée, Baton Rouge, and Manchac. While a few contemporaries first made these charges, local historians were shrill in their later and almost unanimous denunciation of Willing.[33] Recently a few historians, using Spanish sources for the most part, have defended the controversial captain by insisting that his pact with the Natchez citizens applied only to that town and its immediate environs. Therefore the sacking of settlements to the south did not, in the strictest sense, constitute a breach of the original agreement. On the other hand, the decision to continue the pillage all the way to Manchac marked the expedition as one of plunder and indelibly stained the reputation of Willing in the eyes of most inhabitants in the Southwest. Furthermore, the outrageous escapades of these Americans made it all but impossible for the residents of British West Florida to remain as impartial after the coming of James Willing as they had before his onslaught.[34]

If most of the depredations committed by the Americans on their way to New Orleans occurred outside the Natchez District and against individuals who had not taken an oath of neutrality or allegiance, the same cannot be said of Willing's later raids. In fact, William Dunbar, whose recollections provide the fullest evidence in support of the charges against Willing, complained more bitterly about the later plunderings of Willing's men than he had about the initial raids, as terrible as they were. According to Dunbar, Reuben Harrison and Eliot looted the property of men who had been promised "protection and safety" by Willing. "T'would be a prostitution of the name of Americans to honor them with such an apellation," Dunbar acidly recorded in his diary on May 1.[35] These repeated attacks against helpless settlers were far less defensible than the original ones.

Meanwhile, Oliver Pollock was laying the groundwork for the expected arrival of his friend in New Orleans. Since 1768, when he first came to Louisiana, Pollock had assiduously cultivated the friendship of each successive Spanish governor, and he was on especially good terms with Governor Bernardo de Gálvez who had occupied that post since the first of January, 1777. As soon as he received intelligence of Willing's approach, sometime in February, Pollock "immediately waited on his Excellency the Governor & took every necessary arrangement with him." [36] He also dispatched his nephew Thomas Pollock and a party of fifteen volunteers from New Orleans to assist Willing "in capturing the English vessel *Rebecca.*" Although Lieutenant McIntire and his raiders had already accomplished that objective by the time Pollock and his men reached Manchac, the latter gladly cooperated with Willing's party in committing further wrong against settlers on the British side of the river.

Under the urging of Oliver Pollock, Governor Gálvez issued an edict "offering protection to both sides should they flee to the city of New Orleans" and permitting the inhabitants of Louisiana to extend "hospitality and asylum to the refugees." Although this proclamation was ostensibly designed to maintain "the strict neutrality of Spain" towards both belligerents, no one was misled by Gálvez's careful choice of language since his obvious purpose was to allow Willing and his men freedom of the city. On March 1, Governor Gálvez also consented to Captain Willing's request for "permission to quarter some of his people in dwellings in Spanish territory" by offering him the use of a public building as barracks for his soldiers. According to Spanish sources, the governor complied with this extraordinary request out of a "feeling humanity demanded it." Also, "the petitioning men held guns," and Gálvez thought it best to "appease these men, lest they have a pretext to rob and sack the haciendas around about, claiming that hunger or some other necessity forced them." Anthony Hutchins, on the other hand, viewed these proceedings with extreme foreboding. While he was in New Orleans "under parole," he watched in grim silence while Spanish officers engaged in such unneutral conduct "as aiding, assisting, abeting, entertaining, succoring & c. the rebels." [37]

Equally controversial was Gálvez's decision to permit Oliver Pollock to dispose of Willing's plunder in New Orleans at public auction. The governor partially justified this flagrant violation of Spanish law to his superiors in Madrid on the grounds that desperately needed duties would be paid on the "indigo, peltries, etc. which they have salvaged" and that the inhabitants would be able to purchase seasoned black slaves at bargain prices. The most valuable portion of the confiscated property consisted of approximately 680 Negro slaves, most of whom were sold as their former owners looked on in disgust, unable either to prevent the sales or to repurchase any of their more faithful servants.[38]

By early July, 1778, Oliver Pollock reported to the American Congress that proceeds from the auctions had amounted to $62,500, not counting the *Rebecca* which he intended to have repaired and sent out under American colors to join several smaller Spanish vessels in protecting New Orleans against a feared British attack. Equally disgusting to the British Royalists who had temporarily taken refuge in New Orleans was the sight of American "rebels" purchasing arms in various shops throughout the city or seizing "diverse loyal British subjects" and confining them in a guardhouse provided by Spanish officials. Alexander Ross, who lost a ship to these American raiders, testified that he saw two British citizens placed "in irons" and taken aboard the captured *Rebecca*.[39]

The seizures were not limited to persons, however, as small parties of American raiders swept the Mississippi River clean of English vessels as far south as the Balize and committed additional depredations against British settlers who resided just north of Lakes Maurepas and Pontchartrain. A group of twenty-six boatmen, recruited in New Orleans by Captain Paul Lafitte, proceeded down the Mississippi River. After picking up a large number of Americans, they attacked the English brig *Neptune*, anchored near the river's mouth. This vessel was loaded with lumber bound for the British colony of Jamaica in the West Indies. According to four of the *Neptune*'s passengers, they were roughly handled and forced off the vessel and onto a small boat manned by sixteen or seventeen boatmen who were "armed with cutlasses and wore either Cockades or Deer-Tails in their Hats." [40]

On March 24, an armed batteau under the command of Joseph Calvert, reputedly a man of "attrocious character," seized the schooner *Dispatch*, owned by the British firm of David Ross and Company, about four leagues above South West Pass near the mouth of the Mississippi River. The *Dispatch* was carrying a cargo of fifty "Picked Negroes" and one hundred barrels of flour. According to two of the vessel's owners, Calvert, while "pretending to act under the Authority of the Confederate Rebels in the colonies," took their ship to Barataria Bay where he had the cargo unloaded. Two weeks later, Calvert transported the Negroes and flour a few miles north of New Orleans. After disposing of a few captured slaves at one plantation, he brought the rest to Oliver Pollock's estate where, after offering "a parcel of the Negroes for sale," the rebels divided what was left of the cargo among themselves.[41]

Calvert and his cohorts also seized a batteau belonging to Stephen Shakespear of Manchac. Shakespear claimed that his vessel had been taken while it was floating down the Mississippi River by a party of armed men who were waiting in ambush on the property of Joseph Calvert. Willing recounted a different story. According to him, his men first captured the boat in British territory, but it was "stolen Off in the night by Mr. Shakespear contrary to his Faith pledged." Calvert's men later recaptured the vessel on the Mississippi River, "fastened to a Log of wood near the Shore." [42]

For the moment at least, the Americans had caught the British napping and were in command of the situation in the lower Mississippi Valley. The Willing expedition clearly demonstrated the ease with which the Mississippi River could be descended by a foreign nation, and it also exposed to public view the true weakness of the British position along the eastern bank of the river. During the entire Willing affair, Governor Gálvez never waivered from his promised course of favoritism toward the United States. The way now seemed open for the United States to advance in the Southwest if the Congress was willing to seize advantage of these opportunities and if Spain remained constant to her unofficial policy of aiding the American cause.

4

A British
Counteroffensive

INSTEAD of taking up arms against James Willing and the other American invaders, the aggrieved settlers of British West Florida were content at first to seek redress through legal channels. They either complained directly to Governor Bernardo de Gálvez or indirectly to Governor Peter Chester, who in turn forwarded their protests along with his own to Spanish authorities in New Orleans. Without exception the self-proclaimed victims demanded full restoration of all illegally seized property. Governor Chester urged Gálvez to treat Willing and his "Band of Robbers" as common thieves and to punish them accordingly.

The inhabitants of Natchez also hurriedly dispatched an express to Governor Chester asking him for 100 British soldiers, promising in return to erect a blockhouse and temporary barracks to supply such troops with all the fresh provisions they would need. By agreeing to support British troops in this manner, a sizable number of the more prominent settlers at Natchez indicated a disposition, with proper assurances of assistance from officials in Pensacola, to violate the terms of their agreement with Willing and to break their pledges of neutrality.[1]

After consulting with Lieutenant Colonel William Stiell, commander of British forces in West Florida, Governor Chester decided that he could not spare the troops requested by the Natchez settlers. Instead he dispatched the *Sylph*, an armed frigate commanded by Captain John Fergusson, to the Mississippi River with orders to intercept all former British vessels "which the Rebels may have taken in that River" and which they may "attempt to carry out to sea." Chester also instructed Captain Fergusson "to demand restitution from the Governor of Louisiana of all British property brought by Rebels into his colony" and to prevent Gálvez from giving protection to the Americans or from furnishing them with supplies.

Meanwhile, Stiell dispatched an officer and twenty-five soldiers from the garrison at Pensacola to assist Lieutenant George Burdon, commander of the "weakly manned" but armed sloop of war *West Florida*, then patrolling the waters of Lake Pontchartrain. In addition, Colonel John Stuart dispatched seventy-five Rangers and promised later to send an additional force of 1,000 Indians. With the aid of these reinforcements, Lieutenant Burdon was "to secure the Passes" into Lakes Maurepas and Pontchartrain and to ascertain if the Americans planned any further incursions into British territory. If the rebels attempted to cross the lakes, Chester notified Burdon, he was to repulse them.[2]

These countermeasures were less successful than Governor Chester had anticipated and far more provocative than Lord George Germain, the newly-named colonial secretary for the American colonies, wanted. By early March, the *Sylph* had entered the Mississippi River, and on March 14 Captain Fergusson had it anchored "four and a half leagues" off the port of New Orleans. On that same day Fergusson delivered the first in a series of petulant messages to Governor Gálvez. After dutifully conveying to the Spanish governor the substance of Chester's instructions, the captain vigorously protested against the warm reception which Gálvez had given the "body of men who committed depredations" against British subjects. When Gálvez failed to respond to this initial overture as promptly as Fergusson thought he should, the annoyed captain fired off a second note in which he reported a fresh insult "this afternoon from a person who is a Rebel." Lieutenant McIntire, he complained, "placed himself opposite to His Majesty's Ship under my Command and made use of several threats, and provoking speeches, which I forbare to resent, out of respect to your Nation." Before concluding this testy communiqué, Fergusson demanded "full and ample Satisfaction for this Insult . . . to prevent the fatal consequences that may attend your giving more Countenance to a lawless Banditti" than to the lawful subjects of Great Britain.[3]

Highly amused by the McIntire incident, Gálvez acknowledged the justice of Fergusson's demand but chided the irate Englishman for stooping to respond in kind. He would have found the complaint "much more just," the wily governor explained, "if the simple cry which he [McIntire] made to the frigate had not been answered with hard and offensive words." Gálvez considered it absolutely unnecessary for the Englishman to tell the Americans after they had inquired "from whence you came" that "no answers were given to Rebels or banditti." It was only natural, the Spanish governor retorted, for the Americans to have replied that "since we are such, we will come this Night and pay you a visit with two hundred men."

Nonetheless, Gálvez promised that he would compel McIntire to apologize "for having made threats in the territory of His Catholic Majesty as well as for his impudence to you" and suggested that Captain Fergusson detail an officer to receive the lieutenant's verbal apology. Fergusson considered the form of retribution suggested by Gálvez unacceptable and insisted upon having the guilty American delivered to the British for appropriate punishment. Governor Gálvez politely but firmly refused, arguing that since the offense was delivered orally, the response should be in words as well. "If it had been by act, the satisfaction would have been with his person," Gálvez explained. "This is justice, and any other pretension is useless."

As if this patronizing lecture was not enough to ruffle the haughty Englishman, Gálvez, in replying to Fergusson's specific protests, gave the captain additional cause for irritation. He asked Fergusson to quit using the terms "Rebels or Banditti" when referring to "American-Englishmen" who were under Spanish protection. The governor assured Fergusson that, despite McIntire's verbal threat, he had no reason to fear an attack by the Americans. Nevertheless, Gálvez promised to send a boat under Spanish colors with a corporal and six grenadiers to guard the *Sylph* "day and night." As Gálvez expected, Fergusson took offense at this suggestion and informed the governor that he was capable of defending himself and his vessel without the assistance of Spanish soldiers. Not to be outwitted in this exchange of barbed insults, Gálvez informed the annoyed captain that he had never intended to furnish him with a force large enough to protect the frigate, which he knew was well manned, but only one capable of preventing an unnecessary conflict. The Americans, Gálvez explained, respected the Spanish flag.[4]

Even though the Spanish governor enjoyed his verbal sparring with a less talented opponent, the two antagonists soon turned to more substantial issues. Since Fergusson's primary objective was to secure full restoration of all British property seized illegally by the Americans, he cleverly employed some of Gálvez's own words against him. He reminded the governor of his letter of May 12, 1777 to Captain Thomas Lloyd of the *Atalanta* in which he had warned England against seizing American ships on the Mississippi. If Gálvez had in the meantime decided to permit "American Rebels . . . the liberty of committing hostilities" against British subjects, Fergusson reasoned, he could only conclude that "your intentions were hostile to England." For his part, Gálvez was no less firm in maintaining Spain's honor. If Fergusson committed the slightest act of provocation against any resident of Spanish territory "from Manchac to the Balize," the governor warned, "I will be as resolute to the use of arms as I am to preserve the peace."

While steadfastly upholding Spanish sovereignty, Gálvez retreated to a more reasonable position on the question of seizures, thereby postponing an imminent rupture with England. He insisted that in throwing Louisiana open to both English refugees and American patriots, he was merely following a practice common to European nations. Although Fergusson conceded that Americans were received in European courts on equal terms with other nations, he noted that they had never, to his knowledge, been permitted to enter a foreign country armed nor to commit hostilities against Englishmen. In reply, Gálvez contended that Fergusson had misconstrued the substance of his remarks to Captain Lloyd. Since the Mississippi River north of Manchac formed the boundary between Spanish and English territory, Spain could not be expected to prevent seizures there. But south of that line, where Spain controlled both banks of the river, Gálvez acknowledged his responsibilities for protecting all property from illegal seizure or wanton destruction. In fact, Gálvez informed Fergusson, he had already established a tribunal of three Spanish officials to investigate the alleged seizures of private property by the Americans and to compile "a list of the booty taken from the English." When on March 18 Gálvez announced that "there are already various subjects of His British Majesty, who by virtue of Spanish protection have recovered their property," Fergusson interpreted this statement as a pledge that he was prepared to return all English property which Willing and his men had taken in Spanish territory.[5]

As expected, Willing did not yield without strong objections. He thought that several of the seizures were unquestionably legal, even under British law. The *Neptune*, he argued, was captured nine leagues south of New Orleans in the middle of the Mississippi River, where navigation had been freely opened to both England and France. In addition she was on her way to the West Indies "laden with articles absolutely necessary for the Enemies of the States." To strengthen his contention that the *Neptune* was a "Lawful Prize," Willing cited the decision of the British Court of Vice Admiralty at Pensacola which two years earlier had ruled in the case of nine American vessels taken in the Mississippi River that these captures "came under the [same] Denomination as that of prizes made on the High Seas." The vessels of Shakespear and Rapicaut, Willing insisted, were first captured north of Manchac and not in Spanish territory. Futhermore, Rapicaut's boats were engaged at the time of their seizure in illicit trade with "the Enemies of the States of America." [6]

Gálvez remained adamant. He again ordered Willing to return the stolen vessels and their cargoes. In turn, Willing reproached the British for receiving on board the *Sylph* several fugitive slaves belonging to Louisiana planters. Willing apparently suspected that the few English refugees who had accepted Fergusson's invitation of March 23, 1778, "to withdraw to the King's vessel" for protection had recaptured some of their slaves and taken them on board the *Sylph*. On April 1, Gálvez forwarded to Fergusson a list of the missing slaves along with a request for their immediate return. Two days later, Fergusson required those seeking asylum on his ship to furnish him with proof of ownership of all slaves and to put off any Negroes not belonging to them. "We do not wish to incur any suspicion of carrying off the property of a Spanish subject," he explained. On April 12, Fergusson, satisfied that he had no stolen property aboard, set sail for Pensacola.[7]

Meanwhile Gálvez was pleased to inform Governor Chester that he had not only already returned Chester's slaves and those of Philip Livingston, Elisha Hall Bay, Francis Pousette, and William Marshall, but he also had restored David Ross's schooner *Dispatch* and David Campbell's brig *Neptune*, as well as the property of John Priest, Shakespear, William Eason, and Archibald Crawford. But the Spanish governor was smart enough to realize that, as long as Willing and his armed raiders remained in New Orleans alongside the many estranged British settlers who were there seeking refuge or attempting to recover their stolen property, the crisis was far from over. Despite Gálvez's efforts to shore up the city's defenses by setting up a battery of eight cannon along the levee and by launching a galley with two guns mounted on it, the tense situation was hardly eased when the *Hound*, a fourteen-gun British frigate, arrived to reinforce the *Sylph* off the port of New Orleans.[8]

The Spanish governor's apprehensions were further intensified by news of repeated British successes to the north of Louisiana. By the end of April, British troops had regained control of the eastern bank of the Mississippi between Manchac and Walnut Hills. As soon as he learned of Willing's exploits, Colonel John Stuart on Governor Chester's recommendation sent a detachment of twenty Rangers accompanied by Adam Chrystie, a magistrate of the Manchac District, to the Amite River. Chrystie, together with Lieutenant John Pearis and ten Rangers, proceeded to Manchac where, at daybreak on March 15, they surprised a larger force of sleeping Americans. In the process of overunning the "Rebel Guard House," the Rangers killed three persons (including one woman), wounded five or six ("three dangerously"), and took thirteen prisoners before the rest of the startled Americans fled across the Iberville River into the safety of Spanish territory. Too short-handed to retain possession of the fort, Chrystie and his men returned with their prisoners to a more defensible position at the mouth of the Amite River. In April, the Council of West Florida granted Chrystie 3,000 acres of land in recognition of his "noble & spirited behaviour." [9]

In another case of individual heroism, Anthony Hutchins, one of Willing's earliest victims, broke his parole and, with the financial assistance of a few "loyal friends," left New Orleans. Hutchins had learned that Oliver Pollock had dispatched Lieutenant Reuben Harrison and thirty Americans, armed "with some Rifles & the residue chiefly Spanish muskets," to Manchac in a "batteau mounting five swivels." When Hutchins found Fort Bute deserted, he "hastened to the Natchez in . . . Ill state of health." There, with great difficulty, Hutchins persuaded a number of the inhabitants that, since Willing had broken the oath of neutrality, they were no longer bound by it and should join him in preventing further American depredations on their property. With the nucleus he was able to attract behind him, Hutchins and his supporters became less polite and compelled the rest of the inhabitants to join them by threatening to seize their estates and to treat them "as Rebels" if they refused. In the process, the group uncovered "a Rebel's store" where they found "some arms and about 400 lbs of gunpowder which to us was a prize indeed beyond the richest treasure." Armed with these supplies, Hutchins was able to instill greater courage in the frightened settlers, and they began to prepare for an American attack which supposedly was aimed at "robbing the inhabitants of their property without exception."

The unexpected return from New Orleans of William Hiorn, one of the Natchez commissioners, however, threatened to undo much of Hutchins's hard work. Obviously sent north by Willing to make sure that the terms of capitulation were being observed by the inhabitants of Natchez, Hiorn convinced several of Hutchins's more reluctant supporters that the Americans "had not broken one article of the agreement" and that their oath was still binding. In direct contradiction to Hutchins's warnings, Hiorn insisted that Harrison's intentions were peaceful.

After a majority of the more able-bodied inhabitants had deserted him, Hutchins decided to surprise the Americans before they reached Natchez. He posted the few followers he had left at the White Cliffs, about "five leagues below Natchez," where they waited in ambush as Lieutenant Harrison and his men proceeded upstream. However, Hutchins's position was divulged to the Americans by John Tally, who resided a mile below the cliffs. Since Harrison had come to Natchez to enforce the oath of allegiance and not to stir up trouble, he persuaded his informant to return to White Cliffs and inform Hutchins "that he was going to the Natchez in peace."

In a deposition given several years later, William Ferguson, a longtime resident of the Natchez District, remembered that Harrison had instructed Tally to tell Hutchins that, as soon as he arrived opposite the landing at White Cliffs, he would fire a gun. If the English inhabitants "were disposed for peace," they were to signal this intention by firing a single shot in reply. If that were the arrangement, Harrison, by shooting first, provided Hutchins with a perfect excuse for firing upon the Americans with the purpose of either killing them or seizing them as his prisoners. Consequently, Harrison's caution allowed Hutchins to regain the element of surprise which he had lost after his place of concealment had been betrayed. On the other hand, Hutchins was able to report to Governor Chester, with but some degree of truthfulness, "God delivered our enemies into our hands [and] they gave us battle on the 16th day of April last at a place called the white Cliffs."

According to Ferguson, Hutchins urged his supporters to kill the Americans "as soon as they came within gun shot," but the settlers overruled him and insisted that there "was time enough to fire when they found there was a necessity." Although Hutchins sent two of his friends out in a small boat to confer with Harrison, the Americans recognized a trap and ordered "those that were friends to the United States to separate themselves from those that were not." In the confusion which followed, Cephas Kenard, one of Hutchins's more ardent disciples, fired on the Americans, an action which "touched off general fighting on all sides." The advantage, however, remained with the less exposed British sympathizers who hid behind trees and embankments. As Hutchins later informed Governor Chester, he and his men "were so fortunate as to kill, wound or take prisoner every one of them without the loss of a man on our side" and with "but one wounded." The dead included Harrison and four other Americans, while the number of captives came to twenty-eight. Hutchins cut down the American colors and replaced them with "those of His Britanick Majesty" which, he proudly reported, "most splendidly appear in triumph." [10]

As a result of these two uncoordinated events, the British had momentarily regained control of the Mississippi River, but Governor Chester recognized as much as anyone the ephemeral nature of this advantage. After rejecting an earlier request by the inhabitants of Natchez for 100 British soldiers, Governor Chester now accepted a previous offer extended by John McGillivray, one of Mobile's more prominent Indian traders, to raise a provincial corps of five companies (250 men). Chester instructed McGillivray to clear the Natchez District of marauding rebels. As soon as Willing realized that he could not send his captured vessels to Philadelphia by sea, Chester predicted, he and his "Banditti" would try to retake Natchez and attempt to "live upon the Inhabitants as free Booters . . . unless driven out by Savages."

Although he encouraged Colonel John Stuart to dispatch one of his commissaries to the Choctaws for the purpose of organizing a force to assist in keeping the Americans out of the western part of the province, Chester, like many white men, had little faith in the combat skills of Indians. Consequently he was unwilling to place much confidence in their "repeated assurances of Attachment to the King's Interest . . . unless led on by [British] Troops." Afraid that the white settlers of Natchez might flee the district unless it was guarded by British soldiers, Chester urged Major General John Dalling, governor of Jamaica, to furnish him with additional troops and two sloops of war. Chester also requested Brigadier General Augustine Prevost at St. Augustine to send him "whatever assistance" he could spare.[11]

As Chester feared he would, Lieutenant Colonel McGillivray ran into difficulty attracting enlistments even with promises of generous land grants. Although he was able to raise no more than "70 privates [and] most of these in the Natchez District," one company, commanded by Captain Alexander McIntosh, a former member of Stuart's Rangers and another of Willing's victims, was organized in time to assist Hutchins in reasserting British control over Natchez. After their victorious engagement at White Cliffs, Hutchins, who was given the rank of lieutenant colonel, and Thaddeus Lyman, who was awarded a captain's commission, were permitted to raise two additional companies for the defense of Natchez. Most of the volunteers in these units were used to repair and garrison Fort Panmure, while another detachment of 100 men was sent to Manchac to assist in rebuilding Fort Bute and in reasserting British authority over the southern half of the western district.

McGillivray, assisted by Captains McIntosh and Lyman, also collected a force of several hundred Choctaw warriors. By May of 1778, the British Loyalists at Natchez were strong enough to prevent any ship flying the American colors from proceeding up the Mississippi River. As soon as they learned that Pollock was sneaking American goods on vessels flying the Spanish flag, the British began to stop and search Spanish boats as well. Consequently, by mid-May whatever initial advantages the United States had gained from Willing's expedition were completely erased by British countermeasures.[12]

While Hutchins was busy driving the Americans out of Natchez, a new crisis was building up around New Orleans. On April 12, Captain Joseph Nunn appeared off the city's shore in the *Hound*. Captain Nunn found the situation even more critical than he had anticipated. The rebels, he reported, had successfully established headquarters at New Orleans and were sending out "plundering excursions, both by land and

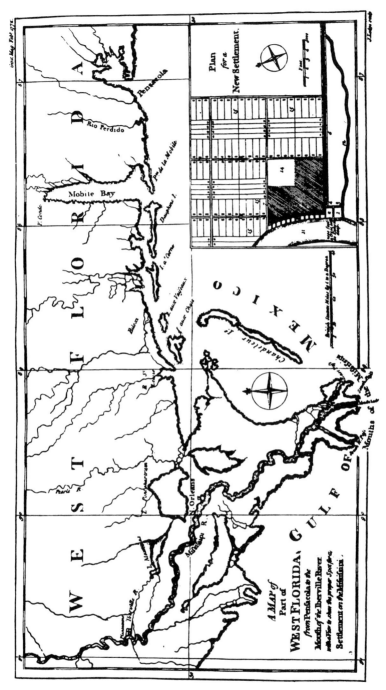

A map of the southern part of British West Florida with insert showing plans for laying out the town of Manchac on the Mississippi River just north of the Iberville River. (Copy in Mississippi Department of Archives and History.)

Lieutenant Elias Durnford, surveyor and engineer in British West Florida. He also served briefly as Lieutenant Governor of the province and was commanding officer of Fort Charlotte when it fell to Spain in 1780. (Copy in Mississippi Department of Archives and History.)

William Dunbar, immigrant from Scotland and early British settler along the Mississippi. Dunbar later moved to Natchez where he became one of the state's most prominent residents. (Copy in the Mississippi Department of Archives and History.)

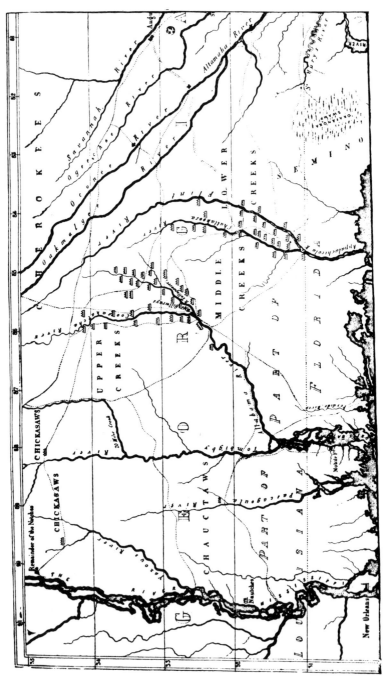

A map of the early Southwestern frontier showing the location of the principal Indian nations. (Original in the Mississippi Department of Archives and History)

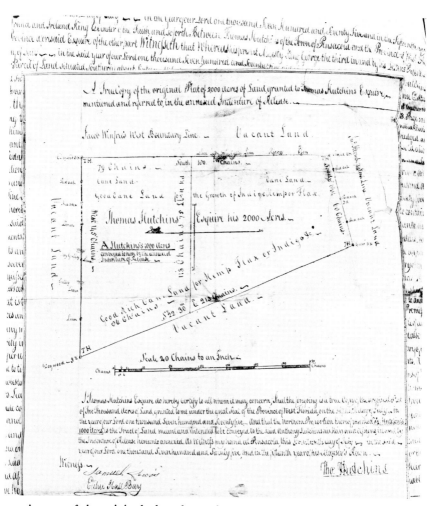

A copy of the original plat of two thousand acres of land granted to Thomas Hutchins in the Natchez District. The grant is dated July 15, 1779. Two other prominent settlers—his brother Anthony and Jacob Winfree—held land adjacent to his. (The original is in the Mississippi Department of Archives and History)

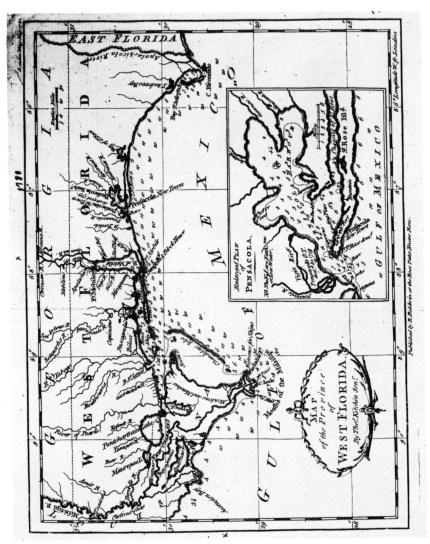

Thomas Kitchin's map of the Province of West Florida with insert showing the harbor of Pensacola in some detail. (Copy in Mississippi Department of Archives and History)

Warping or pulling a flatboat up the Mississippi River. This illustration was taken from a Bank of Mississippi bank note. (Original in Mississippi Department of Archives and History)

Fort Panmure and the town of Natchez in the late eighteenth century.
(From Georges Henri Victor Collot, *A Journey in North America . . .*
Paris, 1826)

water, in so private a manner that it is not possible for the King's Ship's to prevent them." The situation was so distressing, Nunn warned Governor Chester, that "some speedy and spirited measures to prevent a growing evil" were absolutely necessary.

In his negotiations with Gálvez, Captain Nunn was more bellicose and unyielding than Captain Fergusson had been. Although the Spanish governor maintained an outward appearance of confidence and at times even bombast, he was inwardly troubled. Since Captain Nunn was known to be "a brutal man, capable of committing any atrocity without disturbing himself about the consequences," Gálvez expected the worst. He was convinced that Nunn intended "to open fire on the city [of New Orleans] and destroy it." Nevertheless, Gálvez remained steadfast in his determination to protect the Americans and to allow them to retain those prizes which he regarded as legitimate. To continue to do so in the face of mounting British pressure, the governor realized, necessitated additional forces, and he begged his superiors in Havana to send him reinforcements "with promptness." [13]

Of more immediate concern to Gálvez, however, was the large number of Royalists and Americans, "who hate each other to an Excess," in and around New Orleans. Apprehensive lest the British dispatch agents or even raiders into the countryside to win adherents and possibly to foment trouble, Gálvez ordered all "English Royal subjects" who were residing in New Orleans under Spanish protection to assemble at 11 A.M. on April 16 in front of the government house where they were to take an "oath of Fidelity to His Catholic Majesty" not to disturb the peace.[14]

Upon learning of this proclamation, Captain Nunn was astonished. "If your excellence is Alarmed . . . [by] the presence of two British Men of War," he wrote, then "you have it in your power to remedy the effect by Removing from your Province those, who are the Cause of their being here." Although Nunn remained uncertain about Spanish intentions, he assured Gálvez that he was there to protect British commerce from seizure by "Piratical parties fitted out from your provinces" and not, as the governor seemed to fear, to commence hostilities. Gálvez, who actually expected the British to land troops near New Orleans, kept up his bold front and dismissed "these *Men of War*, as . . . [mere] chaloups of War." "They neither alarm nor make me uneasy," he informed Captain Nunn.[15]

Anxious to prolong the negotiations until reinforcements could arrive, Governor Gálvez interjected two unrelated questions into the discussions of late April. He asked Captain Nunn how he felt about Hutchins's escapades at Natchez and about Lieutenant Burdon's unwarranted seizure of two Spanish vessels, both of which were anchored at the time of their capture on the Louisiana side of Lake Pontchartrain. Pleading lack of information and professing to have no jurisdiction over either of the two gentlemen in question, Nunn equivocated on both matters, although he promised to return the two vessels if he should discover that Burdon had taken them illegally.[16]

In the midst of these heated exchanges, another crisis arose to add new fuel to an already simmering fire. Since the outbreak of the American Revolution, the governors of Louisiana and West Florida had employed spies in each other's provincial capitals. After Willing's expedition, however, New Orleans was overrun with British agents, some of whom were merely self-appointed informants anxious to curry favor with Governor Chester or to seek revenge for depredations committed by Willing's men against them. Regardless of motive, all of them attempted to sow seeds of discord among the Americans who were already dissatisfied with their share of the plunder. Hutchins, before he left New Orleans for Natchez, offered a reward of $1,000 for the capture of Oliver Pollock and prizes of $500 each for the seizure of Lieutenant McIntire and Captain Willing. Although Hutchins's clandestine efforts came to nothing, Robert Ross and John Campbell, two British merchants who had fled to New Orleans ahead of Willing, were somewhat more successful.[17]

Along with other British refugees who remained in Louisiana, Ross and Campbell took the oath of fidelity to the Spanish Crown on April 16, although they agreed between themselves to leave the province no later than May 28, when they expected to have all their business affairs completed. Nevertheless, the two merchants grew increasingly indignant over the unnecessary courtesies shown the Americans by Spanish officials. Anxious to disrupt American operations before they seriously damaged the British cause, the two men engaged the assistance of Alexander Graiden, a carpenter who resided in the home of Oliver Pollock. From him, they learned that Pollock had arranged for supplies, valued at 6,000 pounds sterling, to be sent upstream to Fort Pitt. By happy coincidence, Pollock's vessel, the *Speedwell*, was easy to recognize because it had "the Figure of a Woman[']s head at her stern." Graiden also discovered that the cargo included seventeen cases of rifles with bayonets and a large quantity of gunpowder.

Ross and Campbell were anxious to alert their friends in Baton Rouge and Natchez about the Americans' plans, so that they could intercept the *Speedwell* before it reached the Ohio River. The two merchants sent Graiden north with five dispatches, one of which was a letter of introduction to Colonel

Hutchins informing him that the bearer would furnish him with valuable intelligence. Stupidly, they loaned Graiden their horses. When several Spanish soldiers spotted a carpenter astride a fine horse, they grew suspicious and arrested him on May 14, 1778, about twenty leagues north of New Orleans, but not before he had placed all the letters in the hands of William Dunbar. Upon learning that Graiden had been taken into custody, Dunbar hid the letters in a safe place after opening two of them. In addition to the one addressed to Dunbar requesting that he assist Graiden, the other four were intended for John Fitzpatrick at Manchac, Jean Baptiste Tenoir at Pointe Coupée, and Alexander McIntosh and Anthony Hutchins at Natchez.

On May 15, Ross and Campbell were also apprehended and confined, along with Graiden, in a New Orleans jail where they languished without counsel for fifty-five days. The two merchants were at last compelled to pay a heavy fine and court costs amounting to nearly $595 and were banished from Louisiana. Graiden's fate was even more unpleasant; he was sent to Havana where he was thrown into prison for an indefinite period of time.[18]

Even though Graiden never reached Natchez, the purpose of his nocturnal ride was still accomplished. Not wishing to risk further embarrassment by permitting the British to capture a batteau flying Spanish colors and carrying arms and ammunition for the Americans, Governor Gálvez ordered Oliver Pollock to dispatch an express to intercept the *Speedwell*. Fortunately for the governor, Pollock's agent overtook the vessel at Pointe Coupée and brought it back to New Orleans. Since Pollock had incurred heavy expenses in outfitting the *Speedwell* for its abortive journey to the Illinois country, he encouraged Joseph Conard, the *Speedwell*'s captain posing as a "surgeon passenger," to instigate a damage suit against Ross and Campbell after they were released from prison but before they could wind up their affairs and leave New Orleans. By claiming losses totalling $5,900, Conard hoped to refurbish Pollock's rapidly dwindling treasury. Since Pollock expected to send the provisions by way of the Mississippi River "after this blows over," he decided to retain the *Speedwell*'s crew because "Batteaumen and Sailors" of any description were "very hard to get." [19]

Unfortunately for Pollock and Willing, the obstacles they faced did not blow over, and they were forced to devise a different means of transporting Spanish supplies to the American army. Captain Willing by his antics had not only aroused much of the countryside against him, but he had also convinced the British of the need to hasten military troops to the Mississippi and to repair the old forts at Manchac and Natchez. But these British countermeasures were not accomplished without unforeseen difficulties.

To assist Captain Fergusson (who had again sailed to the Mississippi River in the *Sylph*) in transporting supplies to Manchac, Governor Chester dispatched the armed sloop *Catherine* with Lieutenant John Osborne in command. On June 19, while following the *Sylph* up the Mississippi, the *Catherine* struck a large wooden log which tore a deep gash in her hull. Although the crew was rescued by the prompt assistance of Captain Fergusson, much of the cargo was lost when the vessel sank in less than thirty minutes. Through the timely aid of Governor Gálvez, who dispatched a handful of carpenters in two small boats to the scene of the disaster, the British were able to recover a small quantity of provisions which Fergusson hurriedly sent to Manchac. Under the watchful eye of the *Sylph* the remainder of the *Catherine*'s crew, consisting mostly of Germans, stayed behind and tried to salvage the rest of the supplies, which included arms and ammunition, in order to prevent them from falling into rebel hands. Despite these extraordinary precautions, at least one German defected to the Spaniards before the rescue operations were completed. As a result, the troops at Manchac, which included not only the 75 Rangers from Pensacola but also approximately 100 men from Natchez under the command of Colonel McGillivray, were inadequately armed and poorly fed during the course of their stay there.[20]

The situation at Natchez was not much better. A few weeks after Hutchins and his supporters had routed the small party of Americans under Harrison, officers of the provincial forces at Natchez fell into disagreement. British officials at Pensacola had sent Captain Michael Jackson, at the head of a company of Loyalist refugees, to assume command of the hastily organized British troops who were repairing and garrisoning Fort Panmure. Already known to a few of the inhabitants as a horse thief and a scoundrel, Jackson by his high-handed tactics and arbitrary conduct quickly turned a majority of the local citizens against him. Anthony Hutchins, who was in charge of the men prior to Jackson's appearance, collaborated with Captain Thaddeus Lyman and had the obnoxious Jackson arrested.

Lyman, who agreed to take over until a permanent replacement could be named, released Jackson from custody after he promised to resign his commission and to leave the district. Instead of keeping his word, Jackson rallied thirty former supporters to his side, regained possession of the fort, and placed Lyman under arrest. After temporarily losing control of the fort for a second time, Jackson led another successful mutiny and kept the district in turmoil until Lieutenant Colonel Alexander Dickson, the new commandant at Manchac, dispatched Captain Anthony Forster to relieve the crafty Jackson and to restore order at Natchez. Meanwhile, Jackson absconded with as much of the fort's movable property as he could lay his hands on. In the spring of 1779, the two companies of volunteers, commanded by Captains Hutchins and Lyman, were disbanded when British authorities in Pensacola discovered that the units consisted of "few or no men at all besides Officers and Non-Commissioned Officers." [21]

If the British in Natchez were having their troubles, so were the Americans in New Orleans. Although Governor Gálvez maintained a bold front while answering the complaints of his adversaries, he was nonetheless anxious for Captain Willing to depart. When he had originally agreed to assist Willing in the disposal of his plunder and Pollock in outfitting his return to the Illinois territory, Gálvez expected the American visitors to stay no longer than a few weeks. By early April, 1778, Governor Gálvez was doing everything he could to speed Willing on his way, since he realized that the British sloops of war would never return to Pensacola until the American raiders were completely out of New Orleans.

Gálvez's resentment over Willing's protracted stay hardened into anger when the American captain appeared to usurp his authority or tried to question the governor's decisions. Willing attempted to communicate with those prisoners paroled by the Spanish governor through a public proclamation, and Gálvez took him to task for disregarding Spanish sovereignty. Gálvez was equally incensed when Willing questioned his decision to return all property illegally seized in Spanish territory.[22] Since Willing knew that as long as he remained in New Orleans, where he was surrounded by enemies of every description, he was totally dependent upon the governor's friendship, he always backed down and more often than not apologized for his indiscretions. As a result, friction between the two men was kept to a minimum because Willing never allowed it to flare into the open.

The same was not true of the disagreements between Willing and Pollock. While the risk of war with England and the fear of angering officials in Madrid explained Gálvez's uneasiness about Willing's extended visit, conflict over money was the principal basis of contention between the two Americans. Willing and his followers were particularly dissatisfied with the procedure employed by Pollock in dividing up the spoils. Since Pollock did not have enough credit to pay for the numerous commercial transactions authorized by the Continental Congress and the state of Virginia, he hoped to use a portion of the proceeds from the sale of plundered property to discharge some of his overdue obligations. On the other hand, Willing and his men demanded an immediate accounting of the proceeds and full payment of their share of the plunder.

Confronted with daily complaints from his men and officers and with an alarming increase in the number of deserters, which had reduced his party to less than seventy men, Willing vented his anger against Pollock. In late May, he sent a sharply worded ultimatum to Pollock demanding that he "forthwith make out all your accounts so that the one half belonging to me and the men be instantly divided and that you have the Ballance that is due on that Score ready to pay into my Hands on Monday or Tuesday next." Shocked by this "very Extraordinary and unexpected Letter," Pollock promised a speedy settlement, but he reminded Willing that he was largely responsible for the delay because he had failed to place a proper evaluation on the prize *Rebecca*.[23]

Despite the growing enmity between the two Americans,

Pollock remained hopeful of Willing's early departure until the early summer of 1778. On the first of April, Pollock reported that he "was getting everything in order for Captain Willing and his party to set off immediately." Even Willing's protest that there was "no use setting off from here till next Month or even the Month of June" since he could not pass "the Falls of the Ohio till the Month of October" did not completely destroy Pollock's optimism. On May 20, Pollock informed officials in Philadelphia that he expected Willing and his men to "set off from here in a few Days for Manchac where they are going to Entrench themselves till you send down a proper force to assist them in making their Way back." [24]

When the British reoccupied Manchac ahead of him, Willing was forced to postpone his departure once more. By early July, 1778, Pollock's patience had grown thin. He feared that if Willing and his party stayed much longer they would eat up all profits from sale of the plunder. Besides, he bitterly wrote to his superiors in Philadelphia, "the Small party you sent here . . . without any order or Subordination has only thrown the whole river into Confusion and created a Number of enemies." During July, Governor Gálvez also entered the fray and stopped Willing from attacking Manchac after he recalled the *Speedwell* on the grounds that he did not want to give the British any excuse for attacking Louisiana. Thwarted in this attempt, Willing decided to wait for Captain James O'Hara, who was supposedly on his way to New Orleans with dispatches from the American government. O'Hara, however, planned to go no farther south than the Arkansas River. Even after O'Hara failed to arrive in late July, Willing still refused to budge. [25]

By early August, Pollock despaired of ever losing his "old Grievance." "What his next Pretence for tarrying here will be God knows," the dejected Pollock reported on August 11, "but as there is a clear Party to go up, part by Land and Part by Water, . . . and join Col. Clark I am determined to stop all Supplies in order to get him away." This change of tactics produced better results. Sometime in late August, Willing resigned command of his company in favor of Captain Robert George and instructed him to escort approximately fifty of his former men overland to Kaskaskia "by way of Opelousas, Natchitoches, and the Arkansas." Gálvez was so anxious for the Americans to leave New Orleans that he willingly granted Captain George a pledge of safe conduct through Spanish territory, provided he and his men stayed on the prescribed route and promised "not to offend or bother during the journey any English subjects, neither their possessions nor their persons, but on the contrary to treat them with the same consideration as if they were Spanish subjects." The governor also loaned Pollock an additional $6,000 to help defray George's expenses and to outfit the captured *Rebecca* as a ship of war.[26]

George's overland journey was not only expensive but also arduous and full of difficulties. Several of the men became ill along the way, and a small number even died. George also saw his ranks further depleted by desertion. Despite these hardships, Captain George and forty-one of his men reached the falls of the Ohio River in mid-September of 1779 just in time to meet up with the captain's uncle, Colonel George Rogers Clark, who was on his way to Kaskaskia.[27]

Captain Willing and Lieutenants Thomas McIntire and James Eliot were less fortunate. They and eight other companions, two of whom were said to be British deserters, left New Orleans on November 15, 1778, aboard a private sloop which the British overtook at sea. Although all three Americans were taken as prisoners, only Willing was sent to Long Island, New York, where he and the two former British officers who joined him there "found means to make their escape." Willing made his way into New York City and sought refuge in the home of a former friend who was also a British officer, but he "found no Shelter" there. Because he was "a person of Consequence," his friend turned Willing over to British authorities who placed him in irons, to prevent him from attempting another escape. Since Willing maintained that he was a captain in the United States Navy, the British demanded an officer of equal rank in exchange for him, and he was compelled to remain in "this wretched state," which he described as "worse than Slavery," for nearly two years. Although the British for a time held out for Colonel John Connolly, Willing was finally exchanged for a British officer by the name of Rogers on September 3, 1781.[28]

With his capture in late 1778 and his eventual release in September of 1781, Willing's unsavory rebel career came to an end, and the American phase of the Revolution in the Southwest likewise was abruptly terminated. On the other hand, Willing's ill-planned raid on Natchez and Manchac in early 1778 had lasting results for the Old Southwest. Except for momentarily disrupting British trade between West Florida and the West Indies, particularly in lumber and slaves, and except for the small amount of plunder, which totalled less than $75,000 (including the *Rebecca*), none of Willing's other purposes in undertaking the expedition was ever realized. The Mississippi River was not permanently opened to American commerce. In fact, trade on the Mississippi was less accessible to American vessels after Willing's raid than it was before. In addition, Spanish commerce on the river which had been of some advantage to the United States was also disrupted when the British began to stop Spanish vessels and search them for American goods. Furthermore, West Florida did not become the fourteenth American state as many patriots had hoped. Instead, Loyalist sentiment in the Southwest actually increased because of Willing's escapades, which strengthened rather than loosened the ties of many settlers toward England.

In one other particular, Willing's raid damaged the American cause in the Southwest. As a result of it, Oliver Pollock was seriously hampered in his efforts to function as the official agent of the United States and of the state of Virginia at New Orleans.[29] Since much of the plunder eventually went to the men who seized it and since Willing's lengthy stay was more expensive than anyone had anticipated, the American expedition proved to be a serious drain on Pollock's limited financial resources.

George Rogers Clark, who viewed these sad proceedings from afar, succinctly summarized the bitter attitude of many Americans who had once looked upon Willing's expedition with feelings of great expectation. "When plunder is the prevailing Passion of any Body of Troops wheather Great or Small," Clark wrote, "their Cuntrey can Expect but little service from them Which I am Sorry to find was too Much the Case with the party. . . . Floriday on the Mississippi Might have been good subjects to the States if proper Measures had been taken and probably saved the Expence of a Campaign. I should be happy hereafter to find that I am Mistaken on this head." [30] Even if Colonel Clark misjudged the sentiments of most inhabitants in British West Florida, his assessment of Willing's expedition was painfully incisive.

5

A New Belligerent

SMOKE from the fire set by James Willing had barely cleared when conditions in the Southwest began to change dramatically. For months British officials in West Florida, in the Caribbean, and at army headquarters in New York, as well as the king's ministers in London, were concerned that Spain might join France in an alliance against England and in full support of the American rebels. Although a concert of European nations in favor of American independence was illusionary, the threat of Spanish intervention on the side of France in the war against England was,real. Imaginary or not, British officials had to give serious consideration to the possibility that Spain might attack their possessions in the Caribbean and along the Gulf of Mexico.

In New Orleans, Governor Gálvez was well aware of the long-standing British desire to seize the Isle of Orleans and put an end to his clandestine aid to the Americans and his open harrassment of English shipping on the Mississippi River. Like the British who maintained spies in New Orleans to inform them of every suspicious Spanish move, Gálvez employed agents who kept him abreast of developments in Mobile and Pensacola. In fact, Jacinto Panis, a Spanish spy, was in Pensacola when British officials first learned of Willing's expedition. Panis was there to provide Governor Gálvez with detailed plans of British fortifications at those two towns in case war should break out between Spain and England.[1] Despite these efforts, Gálvez was unable to act without the support of Spanish officials in Havana and Madrid, and he waited patiently for the situation to change while carefully planning Louisiana's defense in anticipation of a diplomatic rupture with England.

British settlers along the Mississippi were equally cognizant of the ominous state of affairs in their corner of the world even if they were not as well informed as Governor Chester or the West Florida Council. Rumors of war were omnipresent along the river, and not everyone was as naïve as William Dunbar who recorded in his diary on December 13 that the settlers had "received intelligence of an alliance between Great Britain & Spain." According to Dunbar, Governor Gálvez had confirmed the report which was "an incident very much to be desired by the Inhabitants on this river." [2] Although most Natchez residents desired peace, few shared Dunbar's optimism. In the meantime, it was business as usual for the district's merchants and planters as they resumed their mercantile and agricultural pursuits in a desperate effort to keep from going broke.

Of the three nations involved in the Southwest, England was the first to take positive action to meet the crisis which was rapidly building in late 1778 and early 1779. Although Governor Chester and his advisers were more worried about Spain than the United States, they could not afford to ignore the American threat completely. Throughout the summer and autumn of 1778, British officials kept receiving reports of the approach of an American force larger in size and better led than Willing's paltry band of adventurers. Although satisfied that Willing no longer constituted a serious threat to their security, the Englishmen knew that he had exposed the weakness of British arms in the Southwest and that they must act quickly to shore up their defenses or face the possibility of losing West Florida permanently to Spain or the United States. Consequently they immediately turned their attention to uniting the inhabitants of West Florida, to cementing relations with southern Indian tribes, and to defeating Spanish efforts to attract either or both of these two groups.[3]

As a first step in the execution of this policy, Chester decided to summon the General Assembly of West Florida for the first (and, as it turned out, the last) time during his term as governor, but he and the council postponed issuing the necessary writs until the Mississippi frontier was more secure. Although originally scheduled to meet in Pensacola on June 6, the General Assembly did not finally come together as a body until the first of October, when delegates from the newly created districts of Manchac and Natchez finally arrived in Pensacola. Their tardiness was due primarily to the failure of the writs of election to reach western magistrates in time to hold the elections on the originally scheduled days.[4]

In his message to the General Assembly, Governor Chester, after informing the members of the recent alliance between France and the United States of America, emphasized the urgent need for establishing a well regulated militia and for closer supervision of the Indian trade. In concluding his address, Chester urged cultivation of "union and harmony between the different branches of the legislature as . . . the most likely means of recommending the colony to the favour and protection of government." Although the western delegates, led by the fiery Anthony Hutchins, were eager to enact a militia law, several easterners resented the governor's plea for harmony since they believed that he and the council were actually promoting friction.

A majority of the legislators rallied behind the unhappy

citizens of Mobile who were enraged when the governor in his writs of election lumped their town and Charlotte County into one district, leaving Pensacola as the only town with separate representation. This controversy was just beginning to heat up when "the severest hurricane ever felt or known in this part of the world" interrupted the legislative proceedings for a week. The storm battered the eastern coast of West Florida with "such irresistable fury" that it swept away "all the wharfs, stores and houses contiguous to the water side, [and] . . . part of the front batteries of the garrison, besides destroying several houses and making a general havoc of the fences etc. in the town of Pensacola." In addition, "all the ships and vessels in the habour were either lost, or driven ashore, except His Majesty's Sloop of War the *Sylph*, which with great difficulty rode out the gale." The storm failed, however, to divert the attention of the legislators from the issue at hand or to forge unity in the assembly, and when the members returned to their desks on October 15, the old squabble continued unabated. By early November, Chester had lost his patience, and on the fifth of the month he sent the members home even though they had failed to enact even one of his recommendations.[5]

Unfortunately, the governor's adjournment of the legislature until "the first Monday in September next" did not resolve the controversy. Incensed by Chester's obstinate and arbitrary behavior, a number of legislators, led by Speaker of the House Adam Chrystie and supported by Lieutenant Governor Elias Durnford, drew up a memorial to the king's ministers complaining of the governor's refusal to call an assembly until "a handful of banditti overran Natchez" and, when he did, of his failure to include the town of Mobile in that summons. They also accused Chester of gross negligence for refus-

ing to aid the western inhabitants during the Willing raid and
charged him and his private secretary with misappropriation
of public funds. At a meeting attended by over 100 merchants
and planters and held at the Carolina Coffee House in Pensacola, the governor's enemies entrusted Samuel Hannay, a
prominent western land speculator, with the delicate task of
transmitting the memorial to Lord Germain. Consequently,
at a time when the colony could least afford it (on the eve of
a crisis with Spain), the old feud between the civil and military
authorities of West Florida flared up again. Despite Chester's
denial of the charges, the controversy raged with such inten-
sity that the ministry was forced to begin an investigation
which dragged on until 1782.[6]

Meanwhile, in late March of 1778, George III and his ministers, shocked and dismayed by the news that Willing had
slipped past British sentries and attacked settlements along the
lower Mississippi River, secretly instructed Sir Henry Clinton, supreme commander of the king's forces in North
America, to dispatch 3,000 troops with the necessary arms and
supplies to the two Floridas. Clinton was ordered to send over
half his force to St. Augustine and to send the rest, together
with a general officer who was to assume command of all
British forces in West Florida, to Pensacola.[7]

Although General Clinton was in no hurry to comply with
the king's directives, he finally ordered Brigadier General
John Campbell and 1,200 troops, consisting mostly of German
mercenaries from Waldeck and Loyalists from Pennsylvania
and Maryland, to proceed to Pensacola by way of Jamaica
where they were to pick up additional supplies and the latest
intelligence about West Florida. In late October, after waiting
ten days in New York harbor aboard uncomfortable transport
ships, the men finally embarked for the West Indies. Surmis-

ing that they were heading for Pensacola, the Germans were horribly depressed. In addition to thinking of the long journey before him, one soldier wondered if he and his friends would ever find "their way from there back to the Fatherland." [8]

After a harrowing month-long sea voyage, the British soldiers eventually landed in Jamaica where, within a few weeks, an outbreak of yellow fever nearly decimated the ranks of the more susceptible Maryland Loyalists. In Jamaica, General Campbell received his first briefing on the situation in West Florida. The information given Campbell was "by no means pleasing," but he was in a position to correct only one of the many problems facing him. Learning that troops in Pensacola had never received a daily allowance of rum, a privilege to which his own men had been "regularly accustomed ever since they entered His Majesty's service," Campbell took on board 120 puncheons (approximately 13,400 gallons) of rum before leaving Jamaica. [9]

Expecting to find West Florida "in very great distress," Campbell was not surprised at conditions there when the convoy finally reached Pensacola in mid-January of 1779. "Everything," he reported, was "in a state of Ruin and Desolation." Unfortunately, because the barracks were not ready when they arrived, the British soldiers had to spend ten more unpleasant days aboard their ships before touching land. When the men finally came ashore, they too were dissatisfied with what they saw. "Before us is the Gulf of Mexico, behind us desert regions which are now and then traversed by wandering hordes of wild Indians for purposes of hunting," the German chaplain noted. "For a full twelve miles around Pensacola not a place is seen of which one could say that a stalk of lettuce could grow on it, just nothing but white sand." It had been a good move on General Campbell's part to bring along the rum, for the British soldiers were no happier than the Germans. "I am now in the worst part of the world," one of them disgustedly wrote his friend. The men found it almost impossible to supplement their meager and monotonous rations with a few local delicacies because poultry was "extravagantly dear" and the weather was "so damned hot [that] fish stinks before it can be boiled." According to one disgruntled trooper, the only thing in abundance was "beautiful white sands which circulated freely." [10]

Campbell might have endured the sand and sun with less annoyance if the troops under his command had been well trained, more attached to the Crown, and somewhat more eager to engage the enemy. The German mercenaries were, in the general's opinion, "totally unfit for active service." Their dress, discipline, and demeanor offended Campbell, and he considered them incapable of "acting with that rapidity and spirit . . . necessary to repel an invading enemy [in] . . . the woods and wilds of America." He feared they would easily fall prey to Spanish overtures to desert. The Pennsylvania and Maryland Loyalists repelled him even more. He described them as "composed of the greater part of Irish vagabonds (deserters from the rebels) who from natural fickleness and instability . . . would desert without any other temptation."

As for the troops already in Pensacola, Campbell found the seven companies of the Sixteenth Regiment "almost worn out in the service" and the eight companies of the Sixtieth Regiment filled mostly with "Germans, condemned criminals, and other species of gaol birds." Consequently, Campbell considered all of the troops undependable except for "the veterans of the 16th Regiment." [11] Also at Campbell's disposal were three companies of provincial troops raised earlier by Colonel McGillivray. Upon discovering that they contained almost as many officers and noncommissioned officers as rank and file, Campbell combined all three into one company, which even then contained only twenty-four privates, and placed Captain Francis Miller in command.[12]

Equally distressing to General Campbell was the poor condition of defenses at Pensacola and Mobile. The hurricane of the past October had left "everything in a state of Ruin and Desolation." The scene at Fort Charlotte and in Mobile was no better. "To sum up," Campbell reported, "all the Province of West Florida seems hitherto to have been attended only by false starts, after which every thing was again permitted to fall to Ruin and Decay." To make matters worse, Campbell was caught without the funds, provisions, implements, and laborers required to overcome any of the many problems he found, and he had little hope that the necessities could be procured at any price in the near future. To spare his troops from exhaustion, Campbell asked Clinton to send him a detachment of blacks from Rhode Island to assist in rebuilding the fortifications at Pensacola and Mobile.[13]

Upon his arrival in West Florida, Campbell also found instructions from Lord Germain awaiting him in a lengthy letter dated the first of July, 1778.[14] Germain ordered the general to secure the western settlements from possible American invasion and to guarantee navigation of the Mississippi River for British trade. He specifically instructed Campbell to erect a fort on the lower Mississippi River "capable of being defended by a garrison of 300 men," together with barracks and magazine. Although he left to the general's "Judgment assisted by the Engineer to fix upon the spot," Germain nonetheless recommended locating it "at or near the place where Fort Bute stood." If he found it necessary, Campbell was also to construct "a floating Guard upon that River for the effectual Security and Command of the Navigation." [15]

Since Campbell was in West Florida to secure the province against a rebel attack, Germain cautioned him "to avoid Disputes with, or giving Occasion of Offense to the Subjects of Spain." Consequently, the general carefully kept Governor Gálvez informed of his plans to send a body of troops to fortify the Mississippi and to "protect the Inhabitants . . . from the Insults and marauding Depredations of the rebellious Americans." Under similar restraints from his government, Gálvez was equally cordial and, in the interest of "Friendship and good Harmony," allowed the British to purchase small vessels from Spanish subjects in Louisiana.[16]

Even without Spanish obstruction, the work of fortifying the Mississippi proceeded at a snail's pace. One reason for the delay was General Campbell's personal doubts about locating the principal British fort at Manchac because of its close proximity to Spanish territory, a situation which might encourage desertion. The swampy conditions of the land also made that site extremely unhealthy and difficult to defend. In case the river changed its course, and many thought it might, the fort would be carried away by the Mississippi. Although Clinton was unmoved by these objections, Campbell and the officers whom he had assigned to defend the Mississippi settlements never had their heart in the project. The fort was moved to higher ground, but a shortage of labor, funds, and equipment brought the rebuilding program to a virtual standstill. Furthermore, Indian affairs were also in disarray, largely because of Superintendent Stuart's lingering illness which had prevented him from performing his duties. Even though Stuart's death in March of 1779 was not unexpected, it still left a large void which was not filled until late June when Germain appointed Alexander Cameron to coordinate Indian affairs in the newly created Southwestern District. Word of this decision, however, did not reach West Florida until the end of the summer; in the meantime, Indian relations remained in a chaotic state.[17]

By early March, Campbell, physically weakened by a long bout with ague, was totally exasperated. Exhausted and despondent, he poured out his feelings in a private letter to General Clinton. "I must own," he confessed, "there is nothing I wish so much as relief from my present command finding myself unable to undergo the fatigue and trouble of it, and . . . insufficient for the variety of important business attending it." Two months later, after recovering his health, Campbell had sober second thoughts about this precipitous request and informed Clinton of his firm desire to serve his country whenever needed. In an effort to lay to rest any doubts his superior might have about his character, Campbell assured Germain that he would "repel any descent that may be attempted against this province." Although he concentrated his efforts on the western frontier, Campbell did not completely neglect the defense of Mobile and Pensacola, but progress in rebuilding these fortifications was slow and expensive. While insisting that the forts in both places "must be deserted or repaired," he also pleaded for more protection than the two sloops assigned to the province, neither of which could be "Ranked in the list of the Royal Navy of Great Britain." But Campbell found it nearly impossible to secure naval reinforcements.[18]

Meanwhile, British activity along the Mississippi River alarmed Governor Gálvez. From the meticulous reports of Jacinto Panis, he knew almost as much about the British fortifications at Mobile and Pensacola as General Campbell. Through other sources, Gálvez acquired up-to-date information on the number of British reinforcements sent there in early 1779 and kept abreast of the activities of those troops sent to Manchac shortly after Campbell's arrival in the Southwest. To counterbalance British measures, Gálvez added to his own military strength by requesting a few regular soldiers from Havana and by enrolling new militia companies. By early summer of 1779, the number of troops at the governor's disposal had grown to approximately 800 regulars and 1,500 militiamen, but since Gálvez had to deploy them throughout the province, their effectiveness in defending New Orleans from a possible British attack was reduced.

In addition, Gálvez faced many of the same problems as Campbell. The stockades at New Orleans and the fort at Bayou St. John, north of the city and adjacent to Lake Pontchartrain, were in disrepair, and a scarcity of lumber hampered rebuilding efforts. A shortage of funds plagued Gálvez as much as it did Campbell, and the Spanish governor lamented the "immense cost there has been to the King without putting this place in a state of defense." Although Gálvez was aware of the difficulties the English were encountering in erecting a new fort north of Manchac, he seriously exaggerated their troop strength when in July of 1779 he estimated it at more than 1,000 men.[19]

While hardly unexpected, Spain's declaration of war on June 21, 1779, against England caught British officials in West Florida and Spanish authorities in Louisiana by surprise.[20] Although enlargement of the war grew out of European considerations, Spain's entry into the conflict had the immediate effect in North America of shifting the struggle into the South and Southwest. Termination of the armed truce, which hitherto had hampered the efforts of each European power in the Southwest to expand its possessions at the expense of the other, removed this impediment and provided both of them with a golden opportunity to make their dreams a reality.

From the outset, the advantage lay with Gálvez, since he had advance warning of the impending rupture from his government. Campbell did not know of the declaration until September 9.[21] The personalities of the two principal opponents were even more important in deciding the outcome of the conflict in the Southwest. While Gálvez was bold and decisive, Campbell was cautious and irresolute. As soon as Gálvez was certain that hostilities had commenced with England, he acted with dispatch by taking the fight to the enemy instead of waiting for the reverse to happen.

Sensing in the summer of 1779 that Spanish entry into the war was imminent, Gálvez stepped up the tempo of preparations, especially after intercepting two letters intended for William Hiorn at Natchez. In one of these, Durnford advised Hiorn to be "ready for an expedition against New Orleans in which it is possible that we shall be engaged shortly." In mid-July, Gálvez informed his military advisers of the critical situation confronting the province, but he carefully refrained from informing them of his plans after realizing that they favored a more cautious policy. While ostensibly preparing New Orleans for a possible attack by the enemy, he secretly collected supplies, commandeered boats, and stockpiled ammunition for an offensive maneuver against British settlements along the Mississippi. By early August when he received word from Havana that a state of war existed, Gálvez had concluded, despite the advice of his military council, that the best way to defend New Orleans was to attack Manchac and Natchez before General Campbell and Governor Chester knew of the Spanish declaration.[22]

Gálvez kept these plans to himself until a few days before he was ready to launch the campaign. He originally set August 22 as the date of his departure, but the sudden and unexpected appearance of a raging hurricane on August 18 threw these plans awry. The force of the wind was so strong that trees were uprooted and houses destroyed as far north as 60 miles from the coast, while the heavy rains which accompanied the storm "flooded everything in sight," including Gálvez's immediate plans. The armada of small boats which the governor had been quietly collecting for weeks was scattered, wrecked, or sunk within three hours. As if Providence was entirely against the Spaniards, Campbell and the British completely escaped the hurricane's devastation.[23]

It took more than a hurricane to derail Gálvez from his predetermined course of action. Momentarily distraught, more by the surprise than by the effects of the storm, Gálvez quickly recovered and pushed ahead with his plans. Recognizing the need to circumvent his overly cautious military advisers, Gálvez decided to rally the people to his side. On August 20, he assembled the inhabitants in front of the Cabildo where he painted a gloomy picture of the crisis before them. He told them of England's declaration of war against Spain and of his fears that the English planned to seize New Orleans. Having kept from them the news of his appointment as governor of Louisiana (he was only acting governor before), he publicly announced it for the first time and inquired of the people if he should take the oath. The response was thunderous and infectious. "Fear not taking your oath of office," they cried. They pledged, as Gálvez had just done, their lives and fortunes to the defense of Louisiana. Apparently anxious to attract American sympathizers to his cause, Gálvez on the same day publicly proclaimed, "by beat of drums," the independence of the United States of America.[24]

The governor immediately set the citizens of New Orleans and its environs to work salvaging the vessels damaged or sunk during the hurricane. Gálvez happily discovered that the destruction was not as great as he had first thought. They were able to recover or repair a large portion of the original fleet. On August 27, the governor hurried to the German and Acadian coasts in search of more enlistments while his "small army, . . . [of] 667 men of all sorts and nationalities and colors," followed behind in a somewhat more leisurely fashion.

Oliver Pollock and seven American volunteers accompanied the Spanish troops as they left New Orleans on the afternoon of August 27. This motley assortment of regulars, militiamen, raw recruits, and free blacks and mulattoes trudged "through thick forests and over difficult trails without tents, equipages, or other aid usually considered indispensable, but they marched on as though to happy adventure." By the time the troops reached sight of British Manchac, sickness and fatigue had taken their toll, and Gálvez had lost nearly a third of his men. However, this loss was more than compensated by the addition of the 600 Germans and Acadians and 160 Indians who joined Gálvez's army along the way.[25]

The Spaniards made every effort to keep their operations a secret. On August 29, they seized at Galveztown two British transports which were returning from the Amite River after landing a detachment of Waldeckers there. They later captured a schooner in the Mississippi River laden with rum and other provisions for Manchac and six small vessels, one containing fifty-five German soldiers, on Lake Pontchartrain. Furthermore, Gálvez had both Farquhar Bethune, British agent to the Choctaws who was at Bayou St. John on business, and William Dunbar, who was in New Orleans on a buying spree, arrested and confined to quarters until the governor had returned from his northern campaigns.[26]

Gálvez's deception and cunning, though important, were

not the only reasons why the British were unprepared to meet the Spanish advance up the Mississippi. Part of the problem rested with British officials themselves. In a letter written four days after the Spanish declaration of war, Lord Germain outlined the strategy he planned to follow in the Southwest and the Caribbean. He instructed Campbell to give serious consideration to capturing New Orleans, "an object of great importance." According to British intelligence, Spanish forces in the Crescent City were "greatly inferior" to British troops in West Florida and "the inhabitants generally indisposed to the Spanish government." Therefore, Germain reasoned, the chance of success was excellent if Campbell struck before reinforcements arrived from Havana.

Should Campbell decide to attack New Orleans, Germain authorized him to request naval assistance from Sir Peter Parker, admiral of the British fleet in the Caribbean, and to mobilize the Indians as auxiliary forces. In no case, however, was the general to leave Pensacola unprotected. In his communiqués to other commanders, Germain made it clear that "the first and great object [was] . . . the safety of Jamaica, and next the protection of Pensacola." Sir Henry Clinton instructed Lord Cornwallis, commanding the British army in the Southern District, "if possible to lay hold of New Orleans which would indisputably give us the Mississippi and all the southern Indians." While New Orleans was a desirable target, it was not essential to the success of British arms in North America.[27]

Although Campbell did not receive these instructions until after Gálvez had taken Manchac and was on his way to Baton Rouge, his inclination was toward defense, not offense. He immediately began making excuses and explaining why an attack upon New Orleans at that time was not feasible, even though he appreciated Clinton's point that the crucial question was "whether we are to abandon the Mississippi or get possession of New Orleans." Campbell admitted that to permit the Spaniards to remain "masters of the water communication" was tantamount to surrendering the portion of West Florida which was "of the most real intrinsic value" to England. Campbell justified his indecision by noting the poor quality and condition of the troops under his command. He confessed he had "no confidence in their steadiness, fidelity and attachment." Furthermore, the heat and humidity of West Florida had taken their toll of the men. No fewer than 372 were already hospitalized and the number on sick call increased daily. Desertion remained an even greater problem, primarily because of Spain's willingness to afford the deserters protection.[28]

Despite his own doubts about the success of an offensive operation, Campbell was too good a soldier to disobey the orders of a superior officer. In addition to alerting Lieutenant Colonel Alexander Dickson, commanding officer of British troops along the Mississippi, of the Spanish threat, Campbell persuaded Governor Chester and the council to clamp a tight embargo on shipping out of Mobile and Pensacola in order to prevent "intelligence being sent to the enemy." The general also commandeered all vessels suitable for transporting soldiers. He convinced Chester to detain the packet boat *Carteret* and to employ it in defending the harbor of Pensacola until naval reinforcements arrived from Jamaica. On the other hand, Chester refused to comply with Campbell's request that he declare martial law, on advice of the chief justice who thought it was unconstitutional. The governor did agree to issue a proclamation requiring all citizens to take an oath of allegiance and to enroll as a militia "in case of actual invasion." [29]

While Campbell was securing the provincial capital against a surprise attack and collecting ships and provisions for an assault of his own against New Orleans, the situation along the western frontier rapidly went from critical to disastrous. Developments there eventually forced Campbell to postpone his invasion of the Crescent City permanently. During the late winter and early spring of 1779, Campbell had dispatched Lieutenant Colonel Dickson and some 300 troops, mostly from the Sixteenth Regiment and the Regiment of Waldecks, to protect the western settlements from another raid by the Americans and incidentally to keep a watchful eye on the Spaniards. As the threat of a rupture with Spain grew, Campbell from time to time augmented Dickson's forces with fresh troops from Pensacola, but the combined forces at Manchac and Natchez never exceeded 500 men at any one time.[30]

When Dickson arrived at Manchac in early March of 1779, he found the Mississippi River cresting higher than anyone in the area had ever remembered and just two inches short of spilling over the levee, which the inhabitants had erected the previous winter. Since it was likely that the site of old Fort Bute would shortly be under water, Dickson planned to look for higher ground upon which to build the permanent fortifications. After consulting with two of his subordinates, Captain Francis Miller and Lieutenant John J. Graham (both of whom were experienced engineers), Dickson recommended placing the fort on Stephen Watts's plantation, about 12 miles above the Iberville River. From this vantage point, elevated 20 miles above sea level, the fort could easily command the river for a distance of 8 miles to the north and 5 miles to the south. Since the site was not contiguous to Spanish territory but was "remarkably healthy," desertion and sickness would be less of a problem. By cutting a road through the woods from there to the Amite River, communication with Mobile and

Pensacola could be improved and made less vulnerable to Spanish interference. Furthermore, the natural resources necessary to erect a strong fort were immediately available. Cypress trees were in abundance, and Captain Miller discovered a kiln for burning brick on a nearby plantation.[31]

Unfortunately, Watts demanded such an exorbitant price for the 200 acres required by the military that General Campbell asked Germain to look into the possibility of acquiring a small tract of former governor George Johnstone's vast holdings in the same vicinity. Johnstone's lands were also "high, dry, and healthy." Meanwhile, after Dickson's men encountered severe rains, they were able to accomplish nothing more than to set up temporary barracks and wait for the waters to recede and for replies to their inquiries. It was summer before the terrain was again dry enough to think about construction, but by then the excessive heat curtailed all but light work.[32]

The situation at Natchez was more encouraging. Although Dickson stationed only a small garrison of troops there and Campbell disbanded the remnants of the two independent companies raised earlier by Colonel McGillivray, Fort Panmure was in reasonably good shape. The earlier friction between military and civil authorities had all but vanished, and the inhabitants had returned to their normal routines, hoping that nothing else would occur to interrupt their efforts at eking out a decent living.[33]

Even before the cooler breezes of autumn appeared, Dickson, mistakenly believing that the Americans were on their way down the river, decided to abandon the idea of building a fort in the swampy marshes of Manchac. Instead he moved his men to the healthier and more defensible position on Watts's plantation at Baton Rouge. On July 30, Dickson ordered most of the troops to march northward, after he had sent

Lieutenant Graham ahead with a letter "asking the Inhabitants to cooperate . . . in throwing up a Redoubt which they cheerfully did." On September 3, before the new fortifications were much more than half completed, Dickson learned from a Spanish deserter that Gálvez was on his way to Manchac. Although Gálvez was not aware of it at the time, he had moved at the most propitious moment since Dickson was caught between an indefensible water-soaked fort and an unfinished redoubt. After ordering the destruction of a vessel loaded with provisions for his troops in order to keep it from falling into enemy hands, Dickson began preparing his men to leave Fort Bute permanently and sent word to the laborers at Baton Rouge to complete the new fortifications as quickly as possible. By September 12, the redoubts at Baton Rouge were ready, and Dickson waited anxiously for Gálvez to appear.[34]

Meanwhile, Gálvez had little trouble in taking the weakly defended British fort at Manchac, which he assaulted on the morning of September 7, two days after a force of more than 100 German troops had departed. Dickson had left behind a small detachment of two lieutenants, three sergeants, and nineteen rank and file with orders to delay the enemy long enough to give the rest of his troops time to entrench themselves at Baton Rouge. In the skirmish at Manchac, the Spaniards reportedly killed one soldier and captured two officers and eighteen rank and file. According to Gálvez, an officer and five men "escaped in the imperfect light of a breaking day." [35]

Disappointed that most of the British force had already gone and aware that he had now lost the element of surprise, Gálvez allowed his weary troops to rest from their exhausting march of 75 miles from New Orleans. Since most of his men were civilians and not professional soldiers, they were unaccustomed to that much physical exertion, and the attrition rate was extremely high. After waiting six days for the sick and wounded to recover, Gálvez left Manchac on September 13, arriving at Baton Rouge the next day with 200 men. Along the way he captured five British soldiers, whom he thought were part of an advance guard.[36]

Considering the fact that the British had spent only six weeks erecting the fortifications at Baton Rouge they were still quite formidable. The fort itself consisted of a large earthen embankment surrounded by a dry ditch 18 feet wide and 9 feet deep. Inside the moat was an earthen wall and around its outer edge was "a circle of palisades in the form of *Cabellas de Frisa.*" Gálvez counted thirteen British cannon and estimated the garrison at 400 regular troops and 150 settlers and armed Negroes.

While surveying the terrain and the British fortifications, Gálvez went over his options. He ruled out an immediate frontal assault, such as the one he had employed in subduing Fort Bute, as suicidal and impractical. As he delicately put it, a defeat or a costly battle "would throw the entire colony into mourning." The governor gave some thought to laying siege to the fort and cutting off supplies and reinforcements by blockading the river, but he eventually rejected this strategy out of fear that his small force might melt away before the British capitulated. Gálvez finally determined to open a breach in their walls with his artillery, which fortunately were of higher caliber than the British cannons. The principal difficulty with this option was how to bring up his pieces before the British detected them, a dilemma he eventually resolved by utilizing deception.[37]

Although Dickson had carefully cleared the immediate area of all buildings and debris in order to prevent the Spaniards

from employing them as shelter or cover, the British commander forgot to remove a small grove of trees which reached
out toward the fort. After darkness descended on the night of
September 20, Gálvez cleverly deployed a small detachment
of militia, colored troops, and Indians in the grove as a diver-
sionary tactic. By making as much commotion as possible,
they drew the attention of the British away from the other side
of the redoubt where the Spaniards intended to set up their
heavy artillery "within musket shot" of the enemy. While the
men in the grove either chopped down the trees or threw up
breastworks, others fired on the fort as if protecting these
laborers. The British, "without wounding a single person,"
wore themselves out in a futile all night bombardment of the
wrong target, while Gálvez's regular soldiers installed their
cannons unobserved and unmolested in a garden on the opposite side of the fort.

By morning, the Spaniards had their artillery in place and
ready to fire as soon as the thick clouds which concealed the
British entrenchments from their view had disappeared. Ex-
actly at 5:45 A.M., they commenced a devastating three-hour
bombardment which ripped deep gashes in the British embankments. Although the British, whose cannons were
pointed in the wrong direction, made a valiant and spirited
effort to silence the enemy, Dickson quickly realized the situation was hopeless. At 3:30 that afternoon, he sent two officers
to propose terms of a truce with Governor Gálvez. The astute
Spaniard, who realized he had the British where he wanted
them, would not accept Dickson's offer to surrender unless it
included the fort at Natchez. Knowing that Fort Panmure,
located "in high land," was much more defensible than the
hastily built redoubt at Baton Rouge and anxious to conclude
his Mississippi campaign in order to devote his full energies

to the taking of Mobile and Pensacola, Gálvez refused to negotiate.

Under the circumstances, Dickson had no choice but to accept the otherwise generous terms of Gálvez, who agreed to release all settlers and Negroes, to give the British twenty-four hours to bury their dead without Spanish interference, and to allow the soldiers to march out of the redoubt in full military array—drums beating, colors flying, and under arms—for 500 yards before handing their weapons and flags to the Spaniards and becoming prisoners of war. Gálvez extended the same conditions to the soldiers at Natchez. On the afternoon of September 21, the garrison of 350 men at Baton Rouge formally capitulated and began the long trek south to New Orleans. After dispatching Captain Juan de la Villebeuvre and fifty men north to accept the surrender of Fort Panmure, Gálvez left immediately for the capital of Louisiana.[38]

While the wily Spanish governor had driven a hard military bargain, he displayed his usual compassion toward the civilian population. Two considerations dictated a policy of leniency. In the first place, Gálvez released the civilians because he admitted that "it would have been impossible to guard them anyway." More important was Gálvez's desire to pacify the people with generous terms since he lacked the forces necessary to maintain an army of occupation. He correctly assumed that for the most part the inhabitants would support any government which brought them peace and tranquillity and which did not interfere with their personal affairs.[39]

While Gálvez's army was subduing the English forces along the Mississippi, small parties of Spaniards cleared the British out of Lakes Pontchartrain and Maurepas and the lands around them. With a detachment of troops taken from the garrison at Pointe Coupée, Carlos de Grand-Pré, an enterprising young Spanish officer, seized two small British outposts, one at Thompson's Creek where he took thirteen prisoners and the other at the Amite where he surprised and captured eleven soldiers.

Meanwhile, William Pickles, a semi-literate American ship captain who ran errands for Oliver Pollock, was entrusted with the recently outfitted privateer *Morris* (formerly the *Rebecca*), mounting four two-and-a-half-pounders. Spotting the British sloop *West Florida*, which for two years had ruled the waters of Lake Pontchartrain uncontested, Pickles overtook her and demanded that she strike her colors. When the English captain refused, Pickles opened fire on the *West Florida*, which instantly replied in kind. Somehow, the swifter and smaller *Morris* maneuvered close enough to the larger and better armed British vessel for the Americans to board her. Pickles' men killed four English sailors and forced the rest to surrender, except for one terrified sailor who swam ashore and disappeared into the woods.

Pickles followed up this sensational victory by landing a small force of men on the northern shore of Lake Pontchartrain. On the same day that Gálvez was bombarding the British redoubt at Baton Rouge into submission, Pickles took possession of this territory in the name of the United States and extracted an oath of allegiance from the farmers who resided there. In marked contrast to Willing, Pickles ordered his men to refrain from any plundering, not wishing, as he phrased it in his own inimitable style, to "Mak them ower Inemes." With the concurrence of Pollock and Gálvez, Pickles had the *West Florida* repaired for use in cruising the lakes for "the Common Cause." On September 27, he captured another English vessel containing thirteen Negroes valued at $2,600 off the Mobile coast.[40]

Meanwhile, the inhabitants at Natchez remained completely ignorant of what was occurring to the south of them until early October. On October 2, they learned that Gálvez, with 1,500 men, had assaulted Manchac. The next day, Isaac Johnson, a justice of the peace, received the "dreadful tides" that Dickson "had fallen into the hands of Governor Galvez" and had surrendered Fort Panmure. Johnson, refusing to accept the report as true, went to the Natchez landing on October 4 to find out for himself if the rumors were accurate. Off in the distance, he spotted several barges flying Spanish flags coming up the river. Captain Anthony Forster, commander of the fort, showed Johnson a letter he had just received from Lieutenant Colonel Dickson as well as a translated copy of Pollock's communiqué to the citizens of Natchez. Like many other Loyalists in Natchez, Johnson's response was one of disbelief, followed by anger and disgust. "I am struck dumb," he wrote, "to think of this place being thought so little of as to be trifled away to obtain terms." Johnson was not alone in believing that Dickson had traded away Fort Panmure, the only defensible English fort on the Mississippi, merely to gain more honorable terms for himself and his soldiers. Nor were Johnson and his friends impressed by the reports of Dickson's valor. "In the mighty battle between Governor Gálvez and Colonel Dickson," he sarcastically wrote, "the Spaniards only lost one man and some say not one, the English about twenty-five and the commanding officer wounded in his head by his *tea table*." [41]

The only positive effect of Spanish occupation was to forge unity among inhabitants who had previously been divided into American and British factions. In contrast to the settlers around Manchac and Baton Rouge where animosity toward Spain was not so strong, the inhabitants of Natchez harbored bitter feelings against the Spaniards. When the Spanish soldiers took possession of Fort Panmure on October 5, Isaac Johnson saw tears in the eyes of most settlers as well as "sorrow, rage, and distraction in every feature of their faces." Despite the resentment of many about Dickson's inexcusable conduct, fifty-nine Loyalists of Natchez risked Spanish displeasure to thank the colonel for his "generous and disinterested Attention to our Welfare in the Capitulation of Baton Rouge." [42]

On October 6, many inhabitants gathered at the landing and on the bluff to watch in disgust as Captain Forster and his eighty grenadiers loaded their baggage on waiting barges and left for New Orleans. The British soldiers were barely out of sight when these same citizens began to ponder whether to take the Spanish oath of allegiance or leave the district, perhaps for good. According to the terms of Dickson's capitulation, Gálvez agreed to give those who refused to become Spanish subjects eight months to dispose of their property. Except for a handful who could not abide Spanish rule, most of the settlers stayed on their lands and took the prescribed oath. A number rationalized their decision on the grounds that there was no one to buy their property if they decided to leave. Others insisted that the change of government was only temporary and that British soldiers would return soon. [43]

Meanwhile, the once proud British soldiers, whom Chester now described as "the select and chosen troops of this province," were taken to New Orleans under Spanish guard to await transfer to Vera Cruz. Gálvez gave the captured soldiers freedom of the city and allowed a few officers to visit Pensacola on business. The governor even granted paroles to a handful provided they agreed not to take up arms against Spain or her allies until formally exchanged. Dickson had nothing but praise for the treatment his men received at the hands of the

Spaniards. They were treated "with the greatest Generosity and Attention not only by the Officers but even the Spanish Soldiers seem to take pleasure in being civil and Kind to the prisoners in general." After spending several pleasant months in New Orleans, most of the prisoners (German and British) were shipped on the *Nuestra Señora del Carmen* to Vera Cruz. On August 26, 1780, they were placed aboard the *El Cayman* and transferred to Havana where they remained until the end of the war.[44]

Gálvez's Mississippi campaign was little short of brilliant. With uncommon swiftness, he had rallied a largely alien population behind him, gathered together a motley force of civilian militia and regulars, quickly molding them into a cohesive military force, and then successfully led that force in a campaign which netted the Spaniards 3 forts, 8 vessels, 484 British captives, and almost 1,300 acres of the "best land along the Mississippi." Gálvez had accomplished these feats in less than two months and at a cost of only one man killed and two wounded.

While the British were still contemplating their first maneuver, Gálvez had accomplished the initial stage of his strategy. Throughout, the initiative had rested with him, and England was thrown on the defensive and compelled to outguess Gálvez. Would he attack Mobile first and then assault Pensacola or vice versa? Campbell found himself in a most uncomfortable position, but Governor Chester, although he resented the general's earlier innuendoes against his handling of civil affairs in West Florida, took little solace in his colleague's predicament. Both men now shared a mutual fear for the safety of Pensacola, and not without reason.[45]

While British officials in Pensacola braced themselves for an expected Spanish assault, Gálvez after some hesitation decided to move against Mobile first. Before he could do so, however, he had to overcome the objections of his immediate superiors in Havana who favored bypassing Mobile and proceeding directly to Pensacola. With a logic difficult to dispute, Gálvez argued that "Mobile does not need Pensacola, but Pensacola could hardly exist without Mobile, for from there must come the means and provisions." The disagreement did not prevent Gálvez from proceeding with the attack as originally planned, but it did force him to leave New Orleans with fewer supplies than he preferred because officials in Cuba, largely out of spite, postponed sending them to him. General Campbell, believing that Gálvez intended to strike at Pensacola, refused to weaken his own defenses by sending reinforcements to Captain Elias Durnford who was in charge of protecting Mobile and defending Fort Charlotte, which guarded the entrance to Mobile Bay. Consequently, Durnford was left with a garrison of approximately 300 men, which included mostly slaves and inhabitants and less than 100 regulars, many of whom were ill or convalescing, and without any naval protection at all. Even after the enemy was sighted off the coast of Mobile, Campbell still thought it was a ploy to divide his forces and to weaken his garrison at Pensacola. Consequently, the British general refused at first to send Durnford any help.[46]

On January 11, 1780, Gálvez left New Orleans with some 750 soldiers of all descriptions, only 274 of whom were regulars, and 12 ships, including 2 frigates and 4 brigs. The voyage to Mobile took longer than Gálvez expected. The small fleet first experienced a calm on its way out of the Mississippi River and then had to ride out a violent squall which scattered the ships and almost prevented them from reaching their destination. After regrouping on February 9 a few miles from the entrance to Mobile Bay, the Spanish fleet again encountered rough weather. This time the Spaniards were not so lucky, as seven of their ships ran aground on the sandbars near the coast. Although the British were too short-handed to take advantage of the Spanish misfortune, they momentarily lost sight of Gálvez's ships and erroneously concluded that the invaders had gone home.[47]

Although a lesser man than Gálvez might have withdrawn, the governor inspired his sailors to perform beyond their normal capacities, and, within two days, they had recovered all the battered ships except the *Volante*, larger of the two frigates. Instead of returning to New Orleans as some of his officers advised, Gálvez landed his men at Dog River where he set up camp and made last minute plans for attacking Fort Charlotte which he knew was weakly defended. On February 20, five ships, containing 1,412 men and additional equipment and supplies, arrived from Havana to bolster Galvez's spirits.[48]

On the last day of September, Gálvez opened a correspondence with Captain Durnford looking toward the capitulation of the British garrison and the sparing of the town of Mobile from the ravages of war. Expecting reinforcements from Pensacola, Durnford politely declined both offers and prepared to defend the town and the fort from Spanish assault. During the lull, Gálvez moved his cannon closer to the British fortifications, and Durnford ordered the burning of all buildings near the fort to prevent the Spaniards from using them. Even Gálvez's promise to refrain from erecting batteries behind the charming homes of the town failed to deter Durnford from his predetermined course of action.

On the night of March 9, the Spaniards began opening a trench near the fort in preparation for erection of a battery. When Gálvez decided to continue the work past daybreak, the English opened a withering fire on the men and forced a postponement until nightfall when a heavy downpour accomplished almost as much as British bullets and grapeshot. On March 11, a Spanish scouting party reported seeing fires from two British camps near the Tensaw River and northeast of Mobile. They estimated the combined enemy force at between 400 and 600 men.[49]

These reports were amazingly accurate. On March 6, General Campbell, finally convinced that Mobile was under siege, belatedly left Pensacola with 518 men (413 regulars and militia and 105 Indians) to relieve the beleaguered garrison. Campbell planned to march his forces to Tensaw, a tiny settlement 30 miles north of Mobile, where they were to build rafts and float down first the Tensaw River and then the Mobile River to Fort Charlotte. The British general adopted this course of action as the best way to avoid Spanish detection. On March 10, he accomplished the first part of his objective by reaching Tensaw. His men were busily constructing the rafts and canoes necessary to launch the second phase when the Spaniards discovered them. Off in the distance the British could hear the booming sounds of cannon coming from the direction of Mobile, and they realized that time was against them. On March 14, the firing suddenly stopped, and Campbell feared the worst. Before proceeding any further, the general sent a small party ahead to investigate.[50]

Campbell had not misjudged the outcome of the battle. As soon as Gálvez learned of the British approach, he decided to launch an all-out attack on Fort Charlotte, hoping to subdue it before reinforcements arrived. By ten o'clock on the morning of March 12, Gálvez had his battery of eight eighteen-pounders and one twenty-four-pounder in place and ready to begin the firing. Both sides kept up an incessant bombardment throughout the day. The Spanish fire proved more effective, opening two massive breaches in the British fort, and Spanish provisions were more plentiful, Durnford's men running out of balls of the right caliber to fit their cannon. At dusk, the British hoisted the white flag, and Durnford sent out an officer to propose a truce. Gálvez agreed to stop the firing provided no one left Fort Charlotte and Durnford consented to receive no more reinforcements from Pensacola.[51]

After refusing to accept Durnford's proposed terms of surrender, Gálvez dictated the final articles of capitulation which the British commander signed on March 13. Except for treating the civilian combatants inside the fort as prisoners of war, the terms demanded by Gálvez were strikingly similar to the ones agreed to by Lieutenant Colonel Dickson when he surrendered Baton Rouge and Natchez. At 10 A.M. on March 14, 1780, the "small but brave garrison marched down the breach" and handed their arms and colors over to the Spaniards. The next day, the scouting party sent out by Campbell returned and informed him of the disaster which had befallen British arms at Mobile. On March 15, Campbell's men began the long march of 72 miles back to Pensacola. The British had suffered another stunning defeat in the Southwest, and Gálvez was on the way to becoming the last of the New World conquistadors.[52]

6

---◆◆◆---

An Abortive Rebellion

BY the early spring of 1780, British strongholds in West Florida had been reduced to one—Fort George, which guarded the town and harbor of Pensacola. Although General Campbell expected the Spaniards to launch an assault on Pensacola immediately after the fall of Mobile, Gálvez and his military advisers decided to delay their plans when they learned of British intentions to send naval reinforcements from Jamaica. Campbell took advantage of this unexpected lull in military action to shore up the defenses of Pensacola and to attempt, without much success, to improve relations with neighboring Indians. Unfortunately, both these efforts were hampered considerably when the old feud between the military and civil authorities of the province flared up again.[1]

After a second hurricane dismantled the Spanish fleet in late October and disrupted Gálvez's plans to attack Pensacola, Campbell grew bolder as the Spanish governor became increasingly wary. In early 1781, the usually cautious Campbell went on the offensive. He ordered Colonel Von Hanxleden and a motley force of over 800 men—approximately half of whom were Creek Indians and the remainder a mixture of German mercenaries, American Loyalists, British regulars, and a small number of provincials organized as Royal Foresters—to proceed overland to the Spanish outpost known as

Mobile Village, located on the eastern bank of Mobile Bay. Shortly after capturing Fort Charlotte, Gálvez had established this post, garrisoned by 150 men, as a precautionary measure against a surprise attack.[2]

At dawn on Sunday morning, January 7, 1781, the British surprised the slumbering Spaniards at Mobile Village and managed to penetrate their works before the defenders knew what had happened. In bitter hand-to-hand fighting, the Spaniards pushed the British back and killed Colonel Hanxleden and two other officers. In the utter confusion which followed, the British began a hasty retreat which did not end until they had reached the safety of Fort George. For Campbell the defeat was a bitter one, but he took it philosophically and blamed the miscarriage on "Hanxleden's early fate." [3]

Meanwhile, Gálvez was readying Spanish troops in Havana for a major assault on Pensacola. On March 9, 1781, Gálvez, after two earlier abortive attempts, arrived off Santa Rosa Island, an elongated sandbar which shielded Pensacola Bay from the Gulf of Mexico, with 1,300 Spanish soldiers loaded on twenty-five transports and escorted by a man of war, two frigates, one sloop, and a packet boat. After establishing a battery and encamping most of the men on Santa Rosa Island, Gálvez managed with great difficulty to guide his small fleet into Pensacola Bay before reinforcements, totalling 2,000 men, arrived from Mobile and New Orleans on March 22 and 23. Realizing a frontal assault against the entrenched British was too costly, Gálvez prepared for a lengthy siege.

On March 24, the Spanish governor began the process of ferrying his troops across the bay and setting up a new camp on the mainland below the town. At the same time, Campbell evacuated the town of Pensacola and concentrated his much smaller force of approximately 1,800 men, including Indians, in Fort George atop Gage Hill. Through the remainder of March and during the entire month of April, the Spaniards inched their way closer to Fort George despite repeated sallies from the British and their Indian allies. On the 19th of April, Gálvez saw his spirits further boosted by the appearance of 1,600 fresh troops from Havana. Unless the British navy tried to lift the siege of Pensacola, Gálvez knew it was only a matter of time before the beleaguered Campbell would have to surrender. By early May, Campbell had all but given up hope of naval assistance.[4]

The issue was finally resolved more by accident than by design. After weeks of extensive bombardment by both sides, the Spanish batteries finally found their mark. On the morning of May 8, "as the men were receiving powder" at the Queen's Redoubt on the northwest side of Gage Hill, a shell from one of the Spanish cannons landed at the door of the British magazine. The explosion which followed "reduced the body of the redoubt to a heap of rubbish," killing forty-eight soldiers, twenty-seven sailors, and one Negro and wounding twenty-four others, "most of them dangerously." Although repulsed on their first assault, the Spaniards took what was left of the Queen's Redoubt on their second try. The loss of this position rendered Fort George untenable, and at 3:00 P.M. Campbell raised the white flag and requested an immediate cessation of hostilities. The next day, Gálvez and Campbell agreed to terms, and the British began the painful process of evacuating Pensacola, their last foothold in the Southwest.[5]

While the British were suffering this ignominious defeat to the east, the inhabitants of Natchez were caught up in a disturbance which was not completely unrelated to what was happening at Pensacola. After the Spaniards took over Fort Panmure in early October, 1779, Gálvez launched a pacification program designed to win over the inhabitants and to dispel the widespread notion that the Spaniards treated alien residents harshly. By early 1781, Spanish officials seemed to be meeting with much success in this effort since most of the settlers appeared content and prosperous. For planters along the Mississippi, Spanish rule had several significant advantages since they now enjoyed ready access to the port of New Orleans as well as free and unhampered navigation of the river. Although there was no great reservoir of discontent in Natchez, a number of inhabitants remained loyal to the Crown, and a few looked to the day when England would regain control of the Natchez District. British influence among the Chickasaws and even among some Choctaws was still pervasive.[6]

From time to time, British officials in Pensacola sent out appeals for assistance to Indian allies and white settlers loyal to England who resided in the adjacent countryside. But in each case inhabitants of the Natchez District failed to respond favorably to these overtures. In March of 1781, with the Spaniards at his doorstep, Campbell made one final effort to arouse the Natchez Loyalists to revolt against their new government. By encouraging the citizens of Natchez to throw off the Spanish yoke, Campbell hoped to take some of the pressure off Pensacola where his situation was daily growing more desperate. He notified the settlers that a British fleet was on its way to seize New Orleans and requested their military assistance in recovering Natchez. In order to give their participation the appearance of legitimacy, Campbell sent along five blank captain's commissions to be filled in with the names of prominent settlers who were willing to raise a company of men each.[7]

While the motives of General Campbell in issuing the military commissions were obvious, those of the Natchez fomenters were not so clear. According to Anthony Hutchins, one of the more respected Loyalists in the area, the original idea of the Natchez rebellion of 1781 came from a small group of Americans who plotted to seize the district in the name of England but eventually to annex it to the United States. Realizing that the Continental Congress was in no position to aid them, they decided to approach General Campbell and convince him to assist them.[8]

The principal instigators of this scheme were John and Philip Alston and John Turner, who had originally gotten the idea from Colonel John Montgomery, an officer in the American army. Consequently, the Alstons and Turner dispatched Christopher Marr, "a noted vagabond of bad character & abandoned principles," to Pensacola. Whatever his reputation in Natchez, Marr found a sympathetic listener in General Campbell, who was willing to grasp at any straw in an effort to prevent Pensacola from falling into enemy hands.[9]

Sometime in early April, Marr returned to Natchez with a number of blank commissions, all dated March 17, 1781, and an order for the Choctaw agent to supply him with ammunition. Meanwhile the Alstons and Turner had been sounding out a few prominent Anglophiles to determine if they were willing to support the project, leading the settlers to believe that England would regain control of the district. Upon seeing the commissions signed by Campbell, several of the more reluctant British sympathizers became convinced that the project was worthy of their endorsement. After John Blommart and Jacob Winfree, two prominent men who commanded great respect from the local inhabitants, publicly backed the scheme, most of the other settlers went along with the plans to attack Fort Panmure on April 22.[10]

Despite efforts to keep the project a secret, Alexander McIntosh got wind of it and alerted the Spanish commandant, Captain Juan de la Villebeuvre, who secured the fort and told his men to sleep on their guns. On April 22, when an unarmed force of 200 men, settlers as well as Indians, under the command of Captain Blommart appeared before the fort, de la Villebeuvre tried to turn the attackers back by reminding them of the consequences of their actions. Undaunted by the Spaniard's firm admonition, Blommart ordered the firing to commence. Although the rebel shells caused some damage to the fort, the Spaniards held out for two weeks. The plotters of the rebellion were then forced to resort to deception before they could bring de la Villebeuvre to heel. After intercepting a messenger on his way to Fort Panmure with a note of encouragement from a settler, the rebels sent in his place an imposter, armed with forged papers of identification, and instructed him to notify the commandant that a mine with "combustibles sufficient to blow up the fort" had been deposited beside the structure and to advise de la Villebeuvre that if he wished to avoid further bloodshed he must come to terms with the inhabitants.[11]

The ruse worked. On May 4, 1781, de la Villebeuvre surrendered Fort Panmure and the Natchez District to Captain Blommart. Success bred dissension, however, as the victors fell into disagreement over how to treat de la Villebeuvre and the other Spanish prisoners even before the terms of capitulation were finally negotiated. One group composed mostly of the pro-American faction wanted to take them to Pensacola, but Anthony Hutchins convinced Blommart that those who were anxious to escort the prisoners to the provincial capital intended to murder them along the way. As a result, Blommart agreed to send the Spaniards to Pointe Coupée and to entrust them to the care of those who were most friendly to

England. Blommart later foiled another plan to ambush and kill the prisoners at the White Cliffs.[12]

Meanwhile, the Alstons and Turner expected to raise the American flag over Fort Panmure, but Blommart learned of their intention and hoisted the British colors first. The captain also rejected their idea of dividing the captured stores among the victors. Although the pro-Americans managed to go through the commandant's personal effects, Blommart kept a closer rein on the public stores by appointing a commissary who was instructed to dispense supplies and ammunition only upon the basis of actual need. Blommart further solidified British control over the area by recognizing the civil authority of Anthony Hutchins, who had previously served as magistrate of the Natchez District. Except for a few persons loyal to Spain, the people of Natchez rallied behind Blommart who by then had successfully seized control of the rebellion from the hands of its perpetrators, who were now left without any effective voice in determining the policies of the new government.[13]

The return of British control in the Natchez District was extremely shortlived. Although news traveled slowly in those days, the insurgents of Natchez learned sometime in early May that Pensacola had fallen to the Spaniards. Since Blommart and his supporters knew that the success of their endeavors depended upon British aid, they quickly realized that to retain possession of the fort much longer was futile. Consequently, they made plans to turn the entire district over to the Spaniards under the best conditions possible. They based this decision on their belief that Governor Gálvez, who possessed a reputation for compassion, would treat them as soldiers in the king's service rather than as rebels.

On the other hand, the pro-American faction adamantly

opposed this plan and favored fleeing to the countryside where they expected to hold out until reinforcements arrived from the United States. In the meantime, they urged Blommart to divide the supplies in the fort equally among the participants. The captain refused since he knew that the Spaniards regarded the stores as public property and would treat them as common thieves if they took the provisions. At this point, Blommart wanted nothing so much as to give Spain no further cause for offense. Instead he tried to open up communications with Spanish authorities by sending three emissaries—Alexander McIntosh, William Pountney, and George Rapalje—to New Orleans. Blommart selected these three men because none of them had participated in the disturbance and he hoped that Spanish officials would accept their promises more readily than they would those of the rebels.[14]

On the way down the river, the three were momentarily detained by a Spanish force, commanded by Captain Esteban Roberto de la Morandiere, who was under the erroneous impression that Blommart was preparing to attack Pointe Coupée. After briefly interviewing the trio, de la Morandiere sent them on to New Orleans where they arrived under a flag of truce on June 5. McIntosh, Pountney, and Rapalje described the situation at Natchez as "deplorable" and predicted that the inhabitants would become "victims of the barbarism of these rebels" unless the Spaniards took immediate measures to prevent it. They assured Spanish officials that only a fraction of the population supported the cause of the insurgents and that the vast majority of inhabitants would welcome a return of the Spaniards. In the course of these negotiations, the trio also intimated that General Campbell was behind the rebellion.[15] Spanish officials in New Orleans, however, considered the matter too important for them to decide without first consulting Governor Gálvez who was still in Pensacola. Consequently they instructed Rapalje to return to Natchez and inform Blommart of their decision while the other two emissaries were placed on a ship bound for Pensacola. A few days later, Blommart grew impatient when he failed to hear from the first three emissaries and dispatched Anthony Hutchins and Dr. Francis Farrell with a letter to Governor Gálvez, dated June 2, proposing a return to conditions as they existed before the capture of Fort Panmure. They too encountered de la Morandiere who again refused to have any dealings with Blommart. As a militia officer, de la Morandiere explained, he "could never treat with one who was not only rebel but even a traitor," but he offered them safe conduct on their journey to New Orleans. The next day, June 14, the captain issued a circular to the citizens of Natchez promising not to molest them if they would return to their homes, but he also advised them to fly the Spanish flag in front of their houses.[16]

While de la Morandiere and his comparatively small force of sixty-six militiamen, forty-three Indians, and forty French Canadians slowly made their way upstream toward Natchez, Governor Gálvez returned to New Orleans after demanding that Campbell surrender Fort Panmure, berating him for his part in promoting the rebellion. At first General Campbell denied all responsibility, but he later acknowledged his role in the disturbance after Gálvez showed him not only copies of Blommart's summons to the Spanish commandant but also of the terms of capitulation in which Blommart declared that he held a British military commission. Anxious to protect his subordinates, Campbell then offered to resurrender Natchez on the same terms as Pensacola, "provided that a general Amnesty and Indemnity shall be granted for all past acts whatsoever and that every inhabitant or others in the District of

Natchez shall in every respect be given the same Footing as those of the District of Pensacola." Believing that the Natchez affair was an insurrection and not an authorized military campaign, Gálvez rejected Campbell's logic as well as his proposition. Instead, he cancelled plans to visit Havana and sailed for New Orleans on June 4. Before leaving Pensacola, the governor decided to retain the British general's personal secretary, Major James Campbell, as a hostage; but he permitted the other prisoners to proceed to New York as stipulated by the terms of capitulation.[17]

On June 22, a week after Gálvez had arrived safely in New Orleans, Captain de la Morandiere and his men landed unopposed at Natchez. Although Blommart still hoped the Spaniards would accept his offer to lay down arms in return for a promise of no reprisals against the insurgents, the Louisiana militia officer still refused to negotiate and demanded immediate and complete evacuation of the fort. In response to this demand, Blommart agreed to fly the white flag over Fort Panmure if all the men of the garrison, except for four hostages to be selected by lot, were allowed to return home unmolested. During the same evening that these discussions were taking place, twenty Spanish militiamen slipped into the fort without opposition and took possession. Early the next morning Captain de la Morandiere ordered a detachment of twenty militia, assisted by some eighty inhabitants who had pledged allegiance to Spain, to round up all known rebels in the district while the captain himself placed Blommart, William Eason, Samuel Bingamin, Jacob Winfree, and William Williams under the care of an armed guard for transporting to New Orleans.[18]

In addition to the four hostages taken to New Orleans, the Spaniards arrested a few inhabitants whom they thought were leaders of the Natchez insurrection. However, the vast majority of participants fled into the hinterlands and sought refuge with the Indians. Except for John Alston, the only other persons placed in confinement were British sympathizers who had counted on Spanish goodwill. In fact, few if any of the real instigators of the rebellion were still in the district when the arrests were made. Since most members of the pro-American faction were not permanent residents of Natchez, they had no reason to stay and every incentive to leave.

In addition to the guilty, a handful of innocent persons also suffered. Foremost among these was Anthony Hutchins, who had no knowledge of the plans to attack Fort Panmure until a few hours before the assault began and who later agreed to act as magistrate of the district in order to restore order and keep the peace. Nevertheless, his enemies in Natchez persuaded Captain de la Morandiere that he was one of the prime movers behind the insurrection. Hutchins was forced to leave with his family, and they headed for Georgia. Before they had gone 200 miles, a Spanish messenger overtook them and handed Hutchins a letter of apology from the Spanish officials, "advising him to return and promising him protection." Hutchins agreed to resume his old life at White Apple Village and "things went on well for a short time." But Hutchins was hounded constantly by Spanish officials, who grew increasingly suspicious of his actions, and he once again took to the woods. After enduring untold hardships for several months, he arrived in Pensacola where he secured passage for England on a British cruiser and remained away from Natchez for several years. Hutchins's hasty departure infuriated the Spaniards, who believed he had gone to Georgia to recruit an army in order to recapture the Natchez District. Throughout the summer of 1782, rumors continued to circulate throughout

Indian country that the wiry colonel planned to return with two regiments of soldiers to seize St. Louis, and possibly even New Orleans, as well as Natchez and the Spanish post at the Arkansas.[19]

The bulk of refugees fled either north into Chickasaw country or west into Choctaw territory. The largest colony of these refugees, containing some eighty Americans, sprang up around Chickasaw Bluffs (modern Memphis). "We got all safely to the Chickasaws," John Holston, one of the exiles, wrote his parents; and we "are living all together with Thomas Holmes & wife." A small group of about thirty refugees went to live among the Choctaws, while a dozen or so families made it all the way to British forts in Georgia or the Carolinas. At the time of their departure, Spanish officials made only one attempt to overtake these fleeing settlers. In the fall of 1781, Captain Carlos de Grand-Pré, new commandant of Natchez, sent a small party of Natchez settlers into the Chickasaw towns for the purpose of arresting John Alston and Turner, leaders of the rebellion who reportedly were living in the vicinity. Turner eventually escaped their clutches, going north into the Cumberland Valley, but Alston was not so fortunate. With the aid of some friendly Indians, the settlers seized him, one of his sons, and ten slaves at the Yazoo River. After confiscating Alston's slaves and releasing his son, Grand-Pré brought him back to Natchez and eventually transferred him under guard to New Orleans.[20]

Despite the harsh punishment meted out to a few individuals accused of violating the oaths of allegiance which they had taken to the Spanish government after the surrender of Fort Panmure in 1779, Gálvez treated most of the offenders leniently. The governor later granted a general amnesty which included everyone but the principal leaders of the rebellion.

Although Gálvez considered the conduct of the people of Natchez "infamous, a reflection on all good Englishmen, and a scandal to other nations," he nonetheless decided that, because the effects of the rebellion were insignificant, punishment need not be more severe "than to establish respect for the law, and ought not to extend to any innocent habitants."[21]

After an extensive interrogation of the prisoners, a process which consumed most of the summer and which produced little useful information, Spanish authorities confiscated the property of twenty-one persons including William Eason, John Blommart, Philip Alston, Jacob Winfree, John Turner, and Parker Carradine. The total value of the property was slightly in excess of 15,000 pesos.[22] The Spanish government also kept at least eight of the insurgent leaders in prison and turned aside the pleas of Governor Archibald Campbell of Jamaica, General John Campbell, Colonel Hutchins, and numerous others to have them released. The Spanish also ignored the threat of Farquhar Bethune, Choctaw Indian agent, who promised to "deluge the Banks of the Mississippi with blood" unless "the Natchez Inhabitants" were treated with "Lenity & Compassion."[23]

When all these efforts proved fruitless, James Colbert, the principal champion of the Natchez rebellion, finally converted the numerous verbal threats into reality. Raised among the Chickasaws since childhood, Colbert was more fluent in their language than he was in English. Despite his sixty years, Colbert was still in robust health, blessed with a "strong constitution" that permitted him to endure "the greatest hardships in war." A man of violent temper, he owned a "very fine house, with some hundred and fifty Negroes" in 1782 when he decided to intimidate Spain into releasing the eight insurgents left in prison. Throughout the American Revolution,

Colbert had remained steadfast in his attachment to England and, like his close friends, had cultivated a bitter distaste for Spaniards.[24]

Infuriated by the treatment given Blommart, Alston, and the other Natchez insurgents, Colbert—together with the insurgent Turner—began harrassing Spanish shipping on the Mississippi between Natchez and St. Louis. On April 25, 1782, Turner and fourteen of his compatriots captured a vessel commanded by Captain Eugenio Pouree and disarmed the crew. While being escorted in a canoe to the Chickasaw country, the Spanish prisoners surprised and overpowered their captors. The Spaniards toppled over the canoe and managed to kill six Englishmen and two blacks by beating them over the head with oars as they came up for air. Although Turner was among those thrown into the water, he and one of his slaves recovered the canoe and escaped without injury. Upon learning of the disaster which had befallen Pouree and his men, Captain Grand-Pré dispatched two parties of Indians to bring the English rogues back dead or alive.[25]

The Spanish policy of instant retaliation failed to have the desired effect of either apprehending the culprits responsible for the Pouree incident or detering Colbert and his band of marauders from further aggressive activity. Instead, it stiffened Colbert's determination to undertake additional reprisals against Spanish commerce. Through the assistance of several sympathetic British settlers in Natchez, he learned the contents of almost every Spanish vessel going upstream, as well as the approximate time they were scheduled to pass by Chickasaw Bluffs. Early on the morning of May 2, Colbert and his raiders captured a particularly valuable prize when they seized a boat owned by Silbestre Labadie, a St. Louis merchant, and containing not only a cargo of provisions and 4,500 pesos, but also the wife of the commandant of St. Louis, Francisco Cruzat, and her four sons. As his vessel approached Chickasaw Bluffs, Labadie spotted a boat tied to the bank and, thinking it belonged to a friend, approached it. One of Colbert's men inquired if Madame Cruzat were aboard, informing Labadie that he had some letters for her. The master replied that Madame Cruzat was among his passengers and guided his vessel alongside the moored boat. Labadie was about to leap ashore when some forty men rushed out of a concealed trench near the bank and, with raised muskets, ordered the Spaniards to surrender. "In clear and intelligible French" one of the men cried out, "you are our prisoners, and if you move or shake your head we will fire upon all of you and kill you." The raiders refused to identify themselves other than to say they were Englishmen and to insist that their weapons were their only flag and the powder and ball in their possession were all the orders they needed.[26]

Colbert's men escorted the prisoners, partly by small boat and partly on foot, through a thick underbrush laced with thorns, over rugged hills, across almost impassable streams to a clearing in the interior where they locked the Spaniards in "an uncomfortable, make-shift jail." Although Colbert was openly contemptuous of all Spaniards, he treated Madame Cruzat and her sons with unexpected kindness, although she and the other prisoners watched in dismay as their captors divided the spoils. Colbert and his men began by auctioning off the tableware, then the slaves, and ended up by distributing the guns, clothing, and money among themselves. The next day, some 200 Chickasaw warriors arrived for a major celebration at which they received powder and brandy from the appreciative Englishmen. To the Spanish captives, it appeared as if the Indians were tolerating without approving the escapades of their British allies, although they obviously enjoyed the festivities immensely.[27]

Although Colbert and a few of his lieutenants talked rather freely of their plans with Madame Cruzat and Labadie, they candidly displayed a good deal of uncertainty about how to dispose of their prisoners. The primary purpose in taking Madame Cruzat was to exchange her and her children for the English settlers still under guard in New Orleans. On May 15, Alexander McGillivray, a young half-breed who would one day become the principal chief of the Creek nation, arrived in camp and quickly devised the plan which Colbert eventually used in trying to gain the release of his English friends. McGillivray drew up a "Parole of Honour" in which Labadie and nine other prisoners consented to go to New Orleans and arrange for the exchange after they had pledged to consider themselves prisoners of war and to "return to any of the British Dominions if called upon" before the release took place. Before Labadie left, his captors also forced him to repurchase his own boat "for four hundred pesos" and to ransom "one of his own Negroes" for an additional 250 pesos.[28]

On May 22, Labadie and eleven sailors, accompanied by Madame Cruzat, her four sons, and a black female servant, departed for New Orleans. They carried a letter written by McGillivray, but bearing the name of Colbert, for the governor of Louisiana explaining the terms of their agreement with the prisoners and requesting his immediate compliance. The letter also contained a protest against the practice prevalent in West Florida (especially at Mobile) of "offering Great rewards to Indians for the Heads of particular Men in the Indian Country." On the way down the Mississippi, about "thirty leagues from the entrance of the Arkansas River," Labadie's party encountered three Spanish vessels, one of which was commanded by Colbert's earlier victim, Captain Pouree. Not wishing to risk another capture, the Spaniards immediately returned with Labadie and his party to Fort Carlos III at the Arkansas River where they informed the commandant, Balthazar de Villiers, of the fate which had befallen them. After a brief consultation with de Villiers, Labadie agreed to proceed to St. Louis with a crew made up of sailors from all three boats and inform Lieutenant Governor Cruzat of what had happened. Madame Cruzat and the other parolees were to continue their journey to New Orleans, where they arrived on May 30. Labadie did not reach St. Louis until June 29.[29]

The next move was up to Esteban Miró, who had been acting interim governor of Louisiana since Gálvez's departure from the province in August of 1781. Miró and his advisers carefully pondered the options open to them. They rejected as impractical the idea of sending an expedition to punish Colbert and his band of rogues and to rescue the remaining Spanish prisoners, since the country around the English camps was too rugged and too isolated to undertake such an operation. Furthermore, they were unwilling to run the risk of a rupture with the Chickasaw nation which such an endeavor would probably entail. Miró also decided against attempting to establish a fort at Chickasaw Bluffs since he figured that the insurgents would merely move their base of operation to another spot and continue their harrassment of Spanish shipping on the Mississippi. Instead, the governor resolved to shore up the defenses at Natchez in anticipation of another assault upon Fort Panmure by the English renegades and their Indian allies. Toward that end, he personally went to Natchez with 200 men to supervise the project.[30]

Leaving New Orleans on June 17 with 100 men, Miró arrived at Natchez on the first of July. Finding the fort in a poor state of repair, the governor reconsidered his earlier intentions. He now thought a garrison of 300 men necessary for proper defense of the district and adequate protection of commerce on the river. He also suggested abandoning the posts at Baton Rouge, Manchac, and the Arkansas River and erecting a new one at Chickasaw Bluffs. During his four-month stay in Natchez, Miró continued the policy adopted earlier by Gálvez and sought to win the affections of the inhabitants with kindness. Having already released Parker Carradine and John Smith on the grounds that they had not actually cooperated with the rebels, Miró also freed Mrs. Judith Holston in appreciation of the courtesies shown Madame Cruzat during her period of confinement. Finally, Miró tried to undo the animosity generated by Grand-Pré's decision to impose stiff fines upon the inhabitants of Natchez in an effort to compensate Spain for the loss of ships during the abortive insurrection. On the advice of superiors, however, Miró decided to retain the other alleged insurgents under guard as a precautionary device in case Colbert's men mistreated any of the remaining Spanish prisoners.

On the other hand, Miró refused to negotiate with Colbert on the grounds that he and the other insubordinates were not officially British officers despite the commissions signed by General Campbell. He advised those Spaniards who had signed the parole of honor to disregard it since Colbert was a rebel and most of his followers were traitors. He also refused to discuss any exchange of prisoners with Colbert and continued throughout 1782 to treat Blommart and the others as political criminals and not military prisoners. Although Colbert found the governor's description of the Natchez settlers as rebels amusing when Spain had "Upheld Mr. Willing in Robing & plundering the Inhabitants On the Mississippy

before war was Ever declared," he was unable to prevail upon
Miró to release the English prisoners. Instead Miró insisted
that all negotiations must go through the British governor of
Jamaica.[31]

Meanwhile, Lieutenant Governor Cruzat was undertaking
direct action against the English "pirates." Learning in late
May of the contemplated attacks on Spanish boats, Cruzat sent
a detachment of twenty-five men to protect Labadie's craft,
not knowing that Colbert had already captured it and impris-
oned his family. On June 5, this party arrived at Ste. Gene-
vieve where they received word of Labadie's capture. After
notifying Cruzat of this intelligence, they waited for reinforcements before descending the river to Chickasaw Bluffs.
On orders from Cruzat, they located Colbert's deserted camp
where the Spanish prisoners had been incarcerated and
burned the improvised log jail to the ground before returning
to St. Louis.

The captain of this expedition, Jacobo Dubreuil, later dispatched a party of northwestern Indians into the Chickasaw
territory to recover all Spanish prisoners still left in the area
and to clear out those persons endangering Spanish trade on
the Mississippi. Although unable to kill or capture any of the
English raiders, they located and freed five Spanish soldiers
—one of whom had been a prisoner since early June of 1780—
and one civilian. These same Indians also learned that at least
six Chickasaw chieftains opposed giving further aid and assistance to the English marauders and wanted them permanently
expelled from their territory. Upon receiving news of this
change of heart among a number of prominent Chickasaws,
Cruzat promised to assist all efforts in that direction.[32]

Meanwhile Cruzat incited a sizable party of Kickapoos and
Mascoutens to take to the warpath by informing them that

Colbert and his bandits had seized the ship bringing supplies to them and had distributed the booty among friendly Chickasaws. Those Chickasaw chiefs no longer in favor of supporting the white men who were residing in their country came to terms with Cruzat. In return for Cruzat's promise to prevent the northern tribes from raiding their territory, they pledged to "do everything within their power to expel the bandits from their nation" and to make every effort "to clear the banks of this river of all the evil doers who infest it." [33] As a result of these agreements, Cruzat had seriously undermined the position of the English residents among the Chickasaws.

Despite Spanish policies, which vacillated back and forth between retaliation and conciliation, peace did not come to the Chickasaw country until England and Spain agreed to terms in 1783. For the Chickasaws, the end of armed warfare brought no great joy, since the treaties of peace signed at Paris in 1782–83 had eliminated their ancient allies—the English— from the Southwest and forced them to choose between the lesser of two enemies. Most of them gravitated toward the Americans since they were more like the English, but a fraction, especially the old pro-French group, leaned toward the Spaniards.[34]

During the Chickasaw disturbances, Miró seriously considered moving Blommart and the other Natchez rebels out of New Orleans to a safer prison on one of the Spanish islands in the Caribbean. Learning of this intention, Blommart's daughter made an impassioned plea to Miró to remove her father's irons as "an act of great pity." Before Governor Miró could decide upon either of the two options, the three European belligerents—England, France, and Spain—agreed to preliminary articles of peace in early 1783. With the long war nearing its end, Gálvez who was still Miró's superior determined it was time finally to release "the Chief of the Natchez rebellion" and "his accomplices" from prison in New Orleans as a gesture of friendship and goodwill. Gálvez took the occasion of the arrival of Prince William, Duke of Lancaster, at Kingston, Jamaica where he was to begin his term as governor of that island to announce this decision formally. "I believe, Sir," Gálvez wrote, "that this present is the most appropriate that could be offered one prince in the name of another." Prince William was appropriately grateful. "Your generous conduct," he replied, was "truly characteristic of such a Brave and Gallant Nation as the Spanish." Prince William immediately dispatched the sloop *Heppel* to New Orleans to fetch Blommart and the other prisoners released by Gálvez "on the single condition that under no excuse shall they return to the territory" of Louisiana. On April 28, 1783, Governor Miró, acting under Gálvez's instructions, extended to the six former captives freedom of New Orleans after they agreed not to leave the city without the governor's permission. By early June, Blommart and the five other Natchez rebels were free men on their way to Jamaica.[35]

Unaware of Gálvez's actions in releasing Blommart and the other prisoners and unfrightened by Cruzat's efforts to undermine his position with the Chickasaw chieftains, Colbert continued to harrass the Spaniards. With a force of 100 Englishmen and 40 Indians, he crossed the Mississippi River and attacked Fort Carlos III. Although Captain Dubreuil successfully repulsed the assault, Colbert's men captured Lieutenant Luis Villars and 10 of his men, along with 4 of the leading citizens from a nearby settlement. After a week-long siege of the well-built fort, Colbert retired when he heard that the Spaniards were sending reinforcements, but he took with him Villars, three other soldiers, a son of one of the villagers, and three slaves.

Once more, Colbert tried to secure release of the English prisoners, not knowing that Gálvez had already freed them. This time he sent Villars to New Orleans to arrange for the exchange of Blommart, Winfree, Alston, Eason, and Williams. If they were no longer in New Orleans, Villars agreed to locate their whereabouts and notify Colbert. If he could not obtain their release, Villars promised to surrender himself on August 1 or to pay a ransom of 2,000 piastres. By the time Villars arrived in New Orleans, the English prisoners were at sea on their way to Jamaica.

Governor Miró sent a strong note of protest to Colbert, upbraiding him for undertaking military action after the treaty of peace was signed and demanding that he release all Spanish prisoners still in his custody. In his reply of August 3, Colbert stated that upon learning of the termination of hostilities between England and Spain, he had released all prisoners and had urged the Chickasaws to do the same. He accused Cruzat of failing to live up to his end of the bargain with the Chickasaws by refusing to release the prisoners seized by the Kickapoos during their southern raid. Colbert momentarily broke off further negotiations with the Spanish officials to travel to St. Augustine, where he consulted with Alexander McGillivray on how to treat the recent demands of the governor of Louisiana that he and his men compensate Spain for the damages they had inflicted on Spanish property on the Mississippi. Three days out of St. Augustine, while on his return home, Colbert was thrown from his horse and died before his servant could come to his aid.[36]

By late 1783, the Natchez settlement was again at peace, and the Chickasaw nation had requested the Spanish governor of Louisiana to send them a trader.[37] For the first time in history Spain was in complete control of the lower Mississippi Valley.

7

Epilogue

ALTHOUGH the fall of Pensacola and the resurrender of Fort Panmure at Natchez marked the end of British rule in West Florida, a number of Englishmen familiar with the area refused to accept these defeats as final. A handful of these Loyalists actually devised schemes for the recapture of British West Florida or the seizure of Spanish New Orleans and lower Louisiana, or both. The motives behind these plans were varied, but most of them involved either establishing a haven for destitute and distressed Tories or promoting some new form of land speculation. As an additional inducement to attract the British government's attention, a few of these plotters included plans to retard the growth of the United States. By linking West Florida and Louisiana with Canada, they insisted, the British could erect an impenetrable barrier to American expansion and perhaps suffocate the new republic in its infancy.

For the most part, these plans were based upon the reports of the few Indian commissaries who continued to practice their diplomacy in the Southwest even after the British were chased out of the area and who longed for the return of British control. Almost to a man, these agents commented on the pitiful state of Spanish defenses in the Southwest and the ease with which they could be removed. In fact, Farquhar Bethune in early 1782 requested permission to raise one or two troops of light horse among the Natchez refugees in the Choctaw country to act in concert with warriors from that Indian nation against the Spanish. William McIntosh later echoed these same sentiments when he proclaimed in the spring of 1783, "God send a few frigates round and have that province [West Florida] retaken to make us easy." [1]

One of the earliest of these schemes came from the pen of an Englishman who identified himself by the initials "A. Z." Posing as "an advocate for the Betrayal Loyalists of America," A. Z. proposed reducing West Florida and Louisiana with "a view to provide an Asylum for our unfortunate American Friends as well as to promote the Commercial Interests of this Country." He maintained that a force of 3,500 men, supported by a few British warships, would be sufficient to accomplish these objectives. He also predicted that within a few years "Crowds of Emigrants from the revolted Colonies, seeking, on the fertile banks of the Mississippi, refuge from oppressive Government and heavy Taxes" would populate the region. According to him, "the quantities of Rice, Tobacco, Indigo and Hemp, that might be produced in Soil and Climate so eminently favorable to the Culture of these valuable Articles," would more than compensate England for the loss of her southern colonies. [2]

Even more ambitious was the scheme devised by Lord Dunmore, the last royal governor of Virginia. Returning to America in late 1781, Dunmore landed at Charleston, South Carolina, where he became acquainted with a group of exiles from West Florida which included ex-governor Peter Chester and Alexander Ross. They quickly fell into a discussion of the likelihood of reacquiring West Florida, and they soon convinced Dunmore that it was not inconceivable. The most persuasive spokesman in favor of retaking West Florida as well as seizing Louisiana was Robert Ross. Agreeing in every particular with "A. Z.," Robert Ross, a former New Orleans merchant, also emphasized the desirability of circumscribing the Americans by erecting a ring of British forts from the Great Lakes to the Gulf of Mexico. In addition, Ross possessed detailed information about Spanish fortifications in Louisiana. From John Cruden, British commissioner of forfeited estates, Dunmore gained the idea of employing black slaves and idle white provincials to accomplish his ends. In his letters to officials in London, Dunmore stressed the need for compensating the Tories for their long-suffering loyalty to the Crown and the enormous commercial advantages to be gained from regaining West Florida and conquering Spanish Louisiana. Although Dunmore was not easily discouraged, British ministers were too involved in more important matters to give his scheme or the others any serious consideration.[3]

Meanwhile, Spanish officials worked not only to retain West Florida in the peace negotiations which were taking shape in Paris, but also to secure her possessions in the Southwest from British designs and American encroachments. Specifically, the Spaniards sought exclusive control over navigation on the Mississippi River, removal of Great Britain from the Floridas and the lower Mississippi Valley, and, if possible, confinement of the United States to the territory east of the Appalachian Mountains. To assist them in achieving these objectives, the Spaniards turned to their European ally, France, for guidance and direction. When French officials appeared sympathetic to these Spanish objectives, the three American peace commissioners in Paris grew more and more suspicious of their ally.

At the same time, England came to the realization that American independence was a *fait accompli* and, sensing the growing American uneasiness over Spanish designs, moved to take advantage. She instigated a new strategy aimed at dividing her enemies and recovering American goodwill. As a result, England became more generous toward her former colonies. In preliminary articles signed in Paris on November 30, 1782, between the British and American negotiators, the two countries agreed to mutual navigation rights on the Mississippi River and to the Thirty-first parallel as the southern boundary of the United States. Still England insisted upon including a special provision in the articles which guaranteed that if Great Britain recovered West Florida in the final peace settlement, the boundary would revert back to what it had been at the beginning of the war—"a line drawn from the mouth of the River Yazoo, where it united with the Mississippi, due east to the River Apalachicola." Since England, in another preliminary treaty, ceded West Florida to Spain, this special clause on West Florida was omitted in the definitive treaty between England and the United States signed in Paris on September 3, 1783.[4]

One consequence of this confused maneuvering was that the northern boundary of West Florida was left ambiguous. Although the United States insisted that the Thirty-first parallel was the boundary line, Spain refused to evacuate any of her posts south of Chickasaw Bluffs. In fact, this controversy was not finally resolved until the Pinckney Treaty of 1795 when Spain accepted the American definition. As for navigation rights on the Mississippi, Spain from time to time closed the river to American commerce. Like the boundary question, this matter was not settled until the 1795 treaty.

For the moment, at least, Spain had emerged supreme in the Southwest, and the American dream of gaining a foothold in the area was shattered. Nonetheless, the Spanish hold on the region was as tenuous as British agents had reported, and it was only a question of time before the unfulfilled aspiration of the United States for control of the lower Mississippi Valley was to be realized.

Notes

CHAPTER 1

1. D. Clayton James, *Antebellum Natchez* (Baton Rouge, 1968), 3–12.
2. Cecil Johnson, *British West Florida, 1763–1783* (New Haven, 1942), 1–7.
3. Thomas Hutchins, *An Historical Narrative and Topographical Description of Louisiana and West Florida* (Philadelphia, 1874), 77.
4. Lt. Col. Augustine Prevost to the Secretary at War, September 7, 1763, Report of Major William Forbes, January 30, 1764, all in Dunbar Rowland, ed., *Mississippi Provincial Archives, 1763–1766, English Dominion* (Nashville, Tenn., 1911), I, 136, 113–14.
5. Ibid.
6. Johnson, *British West Florida,* 12–13; Major Farmar to the Secretary at War, January 24, 1764, with enclosure "State of the Revenue of Louisiana, with Appointments Civil and Military, whilst under the French Government," Major Turner to Secretary at War, April 7, 1764, in Rowland, ed., *Mississippi Provincial Archives, English Dominion,* I, 10–12, 30, 116–17.
7. Philip Pittman, *The Present State of European Settlements on the Mississippi* (London, 1770), 78–80.
8. Browne to Lord Hillsborough, July 6, 1768, in English Provincial Records, III, 91–102, Record Group 25, Mississippi Department of Archives and History, Jackson, Miss. (hereinafter cited as English Provincial Records). This letter is also quoted in Clinton Howard, "Colonial Natchez: the Early British Period," *Journal of Mississippi History,* 7 (July, 1945), 163–70.
9. Pittman, *Present State of European Settlements,* 24–25, 78–80; John H. Wynne, *General History of the British Empire in America* (London, 1770), II, 401, 407.
10. Johnson, *British West Florida,* 135–38; Durnford to Chester, June 23, 1771, in English Provincial Records, IV, 663–67; "A Description of West Florida with the State of Its Settlements," Enclosure in Durnford to Dartmouth, January 15, 1774, ibid., VI, 5, 33–34.
11. W. M. Carpenter, ed., "The Mississippi River in the Olden Time: A Genuine Account of the Present State of the River Mississippi and of the Land on its Banks to the River Yasous 1776," *De Bow's Review,* III (1847), 123.

12. Johnson, *British West Florida*, 132–38; James, *Antebellum Natchez*, 14.

13. Johnson, *British West Florida*, 134; J. Leitch Wright, Jr., *Anglo-Spanish Rivalry in North America* (Athens, Ga., 1971), 111–20; Chester to Hillsborough, September 26, 1770, English Provincial Records, IV, 451–68.

14. Johnson, *British West Florida*, 64–65, 135; Browne to Hillsborough, July 6, 1768, English Provincial Records, IV, 451–68; Chester to Hillsborough, September 26, 1770, in Eron O. Rowland, ed., "Peter Chester, Third Governor of the Province of British West Florida under British Dominion, 1770–1781," *Publications of the Mississippi Historical Society*, Centenary Series (Jackson, 1925), V, 20–22.

15. Johnstone to Robertson, February 9, 1765, in Rowland, ed., *Mississippi Provincial Archives, English Dominion*, I, 282; Hillsborough to Gage, April 15, 1768, in Clarence E. Carter, ed., *The Correspondence of General Thomas Gage with the Secretary of State, 1763–1775* (New Haven, 1931–33), II, 61–66; Browne to Hillsborough, August 16, 1768, December 1, 1768, English Provincial Records, III, 115, 221–24.

16. Clinton Howard, "Early Settlers in British West Florida," *Florida Historical Quarterly*, 24 (July, 1945), 45–55; Clinton Howard, "Some Economic Aspects of British West Florida, 1763–1768," *Journal of Southern History*, 6 (May, 1940), 201–21; Cecil Johnson, "The Distribution of Land in British West Florida, *Louisiana Historical Quarterly*, 16 (October, 1933), 639–53. A list of early land grants may be found in Clinton Howard, *The British Development of West Florida, 1763–1769* (Berkeley, 1947), 50–101.

17. Howard, "Colonial Natchez," 156–70; Chester to Hillsborough, September 26, 1770, English Provincial Records, IV, 451–60. The best contemporary account of life in the district is the diary of William Dunbar in Eron O. Rowland, ed., *The Life, Letters, and Papers of William Dunbar* (Jackson, 1930), 23–74.

18. Johnson, *British West Florida*, 136.

19. John McIntire to [Chester], July 19, 1770, Deposition of Daniel Huay, August 25, 1770, copies in Thomas Gage Papers, American series, vol. 95, W. L. Clements Library, Ann Arbor, Michigan; Chester to Hillsborough, September 26, 1770, in Rowland, ed., "Peter Chester," 18–20.

20. Johnson, "Distribution of Land in British West Florida," 539–53.

21. James, *Antebellum Natchez*, 17; W. Magruder Drake, "A Note on the Jersey Settlers of Adams County," *Journal of Mississippi History*, 15 (October, 1953), 274–75; Hutchins, *Louisiana and West Florida*, 43–52.

22. Clarence Walworth Alvord, *The Mississippi Valley in British Politics* (New York, 1959), II, 172–77; Memorial of Major Timothy Hierlichy et al. to Chester, March 5, 1774, English Provincial Records, VI, 119–27.

23. Johnson, *British West Florida*, 139–41.

24. Herbert C. Laub, "British Regulation of the Crown Lands in the West: The Last Phase, 1773–1775," *William and Mary Quarterly*, 2nd series, 10 (January, 1930), 52–55; Jack M. Sosin, *The Revolutionary Frontier, 1763–1783* (New York, 1967), 25–26; Johnson, *British West Florida*, 142.

25. Memorial of Major Hierlichy, et al. to Chester, March 5, 1774, Dart-

mouth to Chester, July 6, 1774, English Provincial Records, VI, 119–27, 141.

26. "A Description of West Florida with the State of Its Settlements," enclosure in Durnford to Dartmouth, January 15, 1774, ibid., 5–6, 33–34.

27. Johnson, *British West Florida*, 143; Petition of James Mather et al. to Chester, April 20, 1774, English Provincial Records, VI, 167–68.

28. Durnford to Dartmouth, January 15, 1774, English Provincial Records, VI, 5–34; Carpenter, ed., "The Mississippi River in the Olden Time," 115–23; Benjamin L. C. Wailes, *Report on the Agriculture and Geology of Mississippi, Embracing a Sketch of the Social and Natural History of the State* (Philadelphia, 1854), 61–62; James, *Antebellum Natchez*, 18–19.

29. Inventory of all the Property, Titles, and Papers of Mr. John Blommart, Seized and Confiscated to the Profit of the King, September 27, 1781, Spanish Record in Natchez, 271–313, Spanish Provincial Records, vol. 17, Record Group 26, Mississippi Department of Archives and History; James Alton James, *Oliver Pollock: The Life and Times of an Unknown Patriot* (New York, 1937), 117–18; Blommart to Pollock, January 7 and 23, 1775, Oliver Pollock Papers in Peter Force Collection, series 8D, Library of Congress; entry of May 1, 1778, diary of William Dunbar, in Rowland, ed., *Life, Letters, and Papers of William Dunbar*, 60–61; Johnson, *British West Florida*, 169, 182.

30. Lucy M. McMillan, "Natchez, 1763–1779" (unpublished M. A. thesis, University of Virginia, 1938), 18–46; James, *Antebellum Natchez*, 19–20.

31. Carpenter, ed., "The Mississippi River in the Olden Time," 121–23; Johnson, *British West Florida*, 157.

32. Carpenter, ed., "The Mississippi River in the Olden Time," 121–22; Hutchins, *Louisiana and West Florida*, 44.

33. Johnson, *British West Florida*, 156–57; Hutchins, *Louisiana and West Florida*, 60–61.

34. William Bartram, *Travels of William Bartram*, ed. Mark Van Doren (New York, 1928), 341–42. For the activities of John Fitzpatrick see his manuscript Letterbook in New York Public Library.

35. Bartram, *Travels*, 335–41.

36. An older study of Louisiana is François-Xavier Martin, *The History of Louisiana from the Earliest Period* (New Orleans, 1882). A more detailed account is Charles Gayarré, *The History of Louisiana* (New Orleans, 1903). The population figures for 1777 are in John Walton Caughey, *Bernardo de Gálvez in Louisiana, 1776–1783* (Berkeley, 1934), 78.

37. The best contemporary account of Louisiana is Francis Bouligny's "Memoirs on Louisiana in 1776," reprinted in Alcée Fortier, *A History of Louisiana* (New York, 1904), II, 25–55. See also Hutchins, *Louisiana and West Florida*, 5–44.

38. James H. O'Donnell, III, *Southern Indians in the American Revolution* (Knoxville, 1973), 5–16; James Adair, *The History of the American Indians* (London, 1775); Arrell M. Gibson, *The Chickasaws* (Norman, Okla., 1971), 66–71; Bartram, *Travels*, 122–24, 153–54, 231–35; Bernard Romans, *A Concise Natural History of East and West Florida* (Gainesville, 1962), 71.

CHAPTER 2

1. Governor Peter Chester to Lord Dartmouth, August 5, December 30, 1775, English Provincial Records, VI, 383–84, 461–62.

2. Chester to Dartmouth, June 9, August 5, 1775, Chester to Stuart, November 17, 1775, Stuart to Chester, August 15, 1775, Chester to Dartmouth, November 18, 1775, ibid., 383–84, 373, 417–18, 421–23, 425–31. See also Philip M. Hamer, "John Stuart's Indian Policy During the Early Months of the American Revolution," *Mississippi Valley Historical Review*, 17 (December, 1930), 351–66 and John Alden, *John Stuart and the Southern Colonial Frontier* (Ann Arbor, 1944).

3. Chester to Stuart, November 17, 1775, Chester to Dartmouth, November 18, December 30, 1775, Germain to Chester, January 25, 1776, all in English Provincial Records, VI, 417–20, 461–62, 395–96.

4. Proclamation of Governor Chester, November 11, 1775, ibid., 451–54.

5. Chester to Dartmouth, November 20, 1775, ibid., 442–50; Johnson, *British West Florida*, 144–45.

6. Johnson, *British West Florida*, 146–47.

7. Chester to Germain, November 27, 1778, English Provincial Records, VIII, 235–37.

8. Johnson, *British West Florida*, 148–49; James, *Antebellum Natchez*, 18–21.

9. Minutes of the Council of West Florida, May 6, 1776, Chester to [Germain] July 1, 1776, Chester to Germain, September 1, 1776, Chester to Sir Basil Keith, September 14, 1776, all in English Provincial Records, VI, 509–12, 542–44, VII, 5–8.

10. Chester to [Germain] July 2, 1776, Charles Stuart to Chester, June 19, 1776, ibid., VI, 515, 517–18.

11. Johnson, *British West Florida*, 205; Chester to Germain, July 3, 1776, Lt. Col. Stiell and Maj. Dickson to Chester, June 25, 1776, English Provincial Records, VI, 527–30.

12. Chester to Germain, October 26, December 26, 1776, English Provincial Records, VII, 36–37, 49–51.

13. James, *Oliver Pollock*, 107; Caughey, *Bernardo de Gálvez in Louisiana*, 86–87.

14. Deposition of Oliver Pollock, June 8, 1808, in James Wilkinson, *Memoirs of Own Times* (Philadelphia, 1816), II, Appendix I. See also p. 150 of Wilkinson's *Memoirs*.

15. Caughey, *Bernardo de Gálvez in Louisiana*, 86–87; Max Savelle, *George Morgan, Colony Builder* (New York, 1967), 175; James A. James, ed., *George Rogers Clark Papers, 1771–1781*, Illinois State Historical Library, *Collections*, VII (1912), 91–93; James, *Oliver Pollock*, 61–65; Unzaga to José de Gálvez, September 7, 1776, in James A. Robertson, ed., "Spanish Correspondence Concerning the American Revolution," *Hispanic American Historical Review*, I (August, 1918), 300–301.

16. Unzaga to José de Gálvez, September 7, 1776, Royal Instructions, December 23 and 24, 1776, in Robertson, ed., "Spanish Correspondence," 301–305.

NOTES 163

For a slightly different understanding of these events, see James, *Oliver Pollock,* 64–69.

17. James, *Oliver Pollock,* 69–70; Savelle, *George Morgan,* 175–76.
18. John Fitzpatrick to Messrs. McGillivray & Struthers, October 31, 1775, Letterbook of Fitzpatrick; Chester to Germain, December 26, 1776, English Provincial Records, VII, 47–49.
19. Chester to Germain, December 26, 1776, Deposition of Charles Roberts, March 28, 1777, Chester to Germain, April 12, 1777, all in English Provincial Records, VII, 49–52, 107–108, 105; Pollock to Andrew Allen and Robert Morris, October 10, 1776, Letters and Papers of Oliver Pollock, item 50, Papers of the Continental Congress, Record Group 360, National Archives, Washington, D.C.
20. Chester to Unzaga, November 4, 1776, Chester to Germain, March 10, 1777, English Provincial Records, VII, 55–57, 99–100.
21. Deposition of William Tracey, December 27, 1776, ibid., 59.
22. Chester to Germain, October 25 and 26, 1776, Germain to Chester, February 7, 1777, Chester to Germain, August 23, 1777, ibid, 29–31, 33–38, 21–24, 189.
23. John Walton Caughey, "Bernardo de Gálvez and the English Smugglers on the Mississippi, 1777," *Hispanic American Historical Review,* 12 (February, 1932), 46–51.
24. Bernardo de Gálvez to José de Gálvez, May 12, 1777, quoted in Caughey, "Bernardo de Gálvez and the English Smugglers," 52–53.
25. British Merchants of New Orleans to Captain Lloyd, April 26, 1777, Minutes of West Florida Council, May 19, 1777, in Records of the States of the United States of America, West Florida, series A, reel 7; Report of Alexander Dickson and John Stephenson, [October 6, 1777], English Provincial Records, VII, 299–302; "An Account of the Interruption to Trade by the Spaniards," n.d., Lt. Col. Stiell to General William Howe, June 3, 1977, Sir Guy Carleton (British Headquarters) Papers, 1747–1783, photostats in Research Department, Colonial Williamsburg Foundation, no. 549, no. 561. The author wishes to thank Dr. Edward M. Riley, Director of Research, for permission to cite the Carleton Papers.
26. Caughey, "Bernardo de Gálvez and the English Smugglers," 52–53; Chester to Gálvez, June 10, 1777, Lt. Col. Stiell to [Germain], June 3, 1777, English Provincial Records, VII, 141–46, 123.
27. British merchants of New Orleans to Captain Lloyd, April 26, 1777, Minutes of West Florida Council, May 19, 1777, Records of States, West Florida, series A, reel 7.
28. Extract from Minutes of Council, June 23, 1777, English Provincial Records, VII, 203–14.
29. Gálvez to Dickson and Stephenson, July 21, 1777, Dickson and Stephenson to Gálvez, August 17, 1777, ibid., 259–60, 269–71.
30. Dickson and Stephenson to Gálvez, August 17, 1777, Gálvez to Dickson and Stephenson, August 26, 1777, ibid., 271–72, 283, 285–86.

31. Gálvez to Dickson and Stephenson, August 26, 1777, Report of Dickson and Stephenson, [October 6, 1777], ibid., 288–89, 295.
32. Caughey, "Bernardo de Gálvez and the English Smugglers," 57–58.
33. James, *Oliver Pollock*, 74–83; Pollock to Commerce Committee, [April, 1777], May 5, 1777, Papers of Continental Congress, item 50.
34. Henry Stuart to John Stuart, August 11, 1777, Rochebleau to Henry Stuart, July 4, 1777, Chester to Germain, August 23, 1777, all in English Provincial Records, VII, 310, 311, 188–89; entry of April 23, 1777, diary of Dunbar, Rowland, ed., *Life, Letters and Papers of William Dunbar*, 46.

CHAPTER 3

1. Savelle, *George Morgan*, 175–76; Moreau B. C. Chambers, "History of Fort Panmure at Natchez, 1763–1785" (M. A. thesis, Duke University, 1942), 83–85; George Morgan to Gálvez, April 22, 1777, Spanish Provincial Records, X, 72–77 (this letter is also quoted in Charles Gayarré, *History of Louisiana, The Spanish Dominion* (New York, 1854), III, 109–10).
2. Gálvez to Morgan, August 9, 1777, in Robertson, ed., "Spanish Correspondence," 308–10.
3. Savelle, *George Morgan*, 177–78; "Plan proposed for an Expedition against West Florida," enclosure in Memorandum, George Morgan to General Benedict Arnold, June 28, 1777, Arnold to Richard Peters, July 5, 1777, Morgan to Arnold, June 28, 1777, Papers of Continental Congress, item 147, I, 253–61, 263–70.
4. Worthington C. Ford et al., eds., *Journals of the Continental Congress, 1774–1789* (Washington, D.C., 1904–37), VIII, 566–67.
5. Charles Thompson, notes on debates in Congress, in Edmund C. Burnett, ed., *Letters of Members of the Continental Congress* (Washington, D.C., 1921–36), II, 421–22.
6. Henry Laurens to Lachlan McIntosh, August 11, 1777, Laurens to the President of South Carolina, August 12, 1777, ibid., 443–47.
7. Commerce Committee to Pollock, November 21, 1777, General Edward Hand to Board of War, February 12, 1778, Papers of Continental Congress, items 50 and 159; Ford et al., eds., *Journals of the Continental Congress*, X, 106, 184. On the operations of the Commerce Committee, see Edmund C. Burnett, *The Continental Congress: A Definitive History of the Continental Congress from its Inception in 1774 to March, 1789* (New York, 1941), 118–19.
8. There is very little information on the early life of James Willing. The extensive Willing family papers in the Historical Society of Pennsylvania contain only a few references to him, and the most recent study of his brother's financial operations fails to mention him—Burton Alva Konkle, *Thomas Willing and the First American Financial System* (Philadelphia, 1937). There are a few references to James Willing, mostly about his indebtedness, in the Pollock papers in the Library of Congress. Some information on his career in the Southwest is in John Walton Caughey, "Willing's Expedition Down the Mississippi, 1778," *Louisiana Historical Quarterly*, 15 (January, 1932),

5–6, and Robert V. Haynes, "James Willing and the Planters of Natchez: The American Revolution Comes to the Southwest," *Journal of Mississippi History,* 37 (February, 1975), 4–5. On May 4 and 5, 1777, Pollock wrote letters to two of his friends on the secret committee. See Secret Committee to Pollock, June 12, 1777, Burnett, ed., *Letters,* II, 380.

9. Minutes of West Florida Council, August 4 and November 2, 1772, and September 23, 1773, Records of States, West Florida, series A, reel 4; Pollock to Haldimand, December 1, 1772, Willing to Haldimand, November 11, 1772, quoted in James, *Oliver Pollock,* 117–18; entry of May 1, 1778, in Rowland, ed., *Life, Letters, and Papers of William Dunbar,* 60–66.

10. J. F. H. Claiborne, *Mississippi; as a Province, Territory, and State* (Jackson, 1880), 117; Caughey, *Bernardo de Gálvez in Louisiana,* 103; Memorial of James Willing to Congress, October 29, 1781, Papers of the Continental Congress, item 42, VIII, 237–39.

11. Commerce Committee to Edward Hand, November 21, 1777, Burnett, ed., *Letters,* II, 565; Memorial of James Willing to Congress, October 29, 1781, Papers of the Continental Congress, item 42, VIII, 237–39.

12. Pollock to Commerce Committee, March 6, 1778, Papers of the Continental Congress, item 50; General Edward Hand to Secretary of War, December 24, 1777, in Reuben Gold Thwaites and Louise Phelps Kellogg, eds., *Frontier Defense on the Upper Ohio, 1777–1779* (Madison, 1912), 191–92; Morgan to Willing, January, 1778, General Edward Hand Papers in Simon Gratz Autograph Collection, Historical Society of Pennsylvania, Philadelphia, Pa.

13. Return of volunteer crew of *Rattletrap* under Capt. Jas. Willing, December 22, 1777, in Kellogg and Thwaites, eds., *Frontier Defense,* 302–303; Memorial of Thomas McIntire to Board of War, January 23, 1779, Commerce Committee to Pollock, November 21, 1777, Papers of the Continental Congress, items 41, VI and 50; Ford, ed., *Journals of the Continental Congress,* XIII, 291–92; James Willing to General Hand, January 7, 1778, Morgan to Willing, January, 1778, General Edward Hand Papers.

14. Caughey, *Bernardo de Gálvez in Louisiana,* 105–106; Thwaites and Kellogg, eds., *Frontier Defense,* 287–88; Clark's Memoirs, 1773–1779; Willing to Clark, September 1, 1778, James, ed., *George Rogers Clark Papers,* 225, 67–68; Cruzat to Morgan, November 19, 1777, Papers of the Continental Congress, item 78, V, 109–21; Burnett, ed., *Letters,* III, 144 *n.*

15. Hardy Perry to [Farquhar Bethune], February 4, 1778, Carleton Papers, no. 920; Fitzpatrick to John Miller, October 6, 1777, Letterbook of Fitzpatrick; Joseph Barton Starr, "Tories, Dons, and Rebels: The American Revolution in British West Florida" (unpublished Ph. D. dissertation, Florida State University, 1971), 150.

16. Petition of fourteen Americans, February 2, 1778, quoted in Caughey, *Bernardo de Gálvez in Louisiana,* 106; Fitzpatrick to Michael Hooppock, July 8, 1777, Fitzpatrick Letterbook; Chester to Germain, January 16, March 25, 1778, English Provincial Records, VII, 327–28, 347–48; Stuart to Howe, March 22, 1778, in Clinton Papers.

17. Chester to Germain, March 25, 1778, English Provincial Records,

VII, 347–48; Perry to [Bethune], February 4, 1778, Carleton Papers, no. 920.

18. Starr, "Dons, Tories, and Rebels," 152–53; Chester to Germain, March 25, 1778, English Provincial Records, VII, 348; Minutes of West Florida Council, March 5, 1778, Records of States, West Florida, series A, reel 8; James Willing to Commerce Committee, April 14, 1778, Papers of Continental Congress, item 78, XXIII, 491.

19. Testimony of Alexander McIntosh, Minutes of West Florida Council, March 17, 1778, Records of States, West Florida, series A, reel 8.

20. Anonymous to John Campbell, March 1, 1778, Minutes of West Florida Council, March 18, 1778, Testimony of Alexander McIntosh, Minutes of West Florida Council, March 17, 1778, ibid. See also G. Douglas Inglis, "Anthony Hutchins: Early Natchez Planter" (unpublished M. A. thesis, University of Southern Mississippi, 1973).

21. Deposition of William Ferguson, November 6, 1797, quoted in Andrew Ellicott, *The Journal of Andrew Ellicott* (Chicago, 1962), 130; John Q. Anderson, ed., "The Narrative of John Hutchins," *Journal of Mississippi History*, 20 (January, 1958), 8–9; Hutchins to Germain, May 21, 1778, English Provincial Records, VII, 381; Claiborne, *Mississippi*, 118.

22. Testimony of Joseph Dawes, Minutes of West Florida Council, March 10, 1778, Testimony of Thomas Gibson, Minutes of West Florida Council, March 18, 1778, Records of States, West Florida, series A, reel 8.

23. William Hiorn, Richard Ellis and Joseph Thompson to the Governor, February 23, 1778, Minutes of West Florida Council, May 7, 1778, ibid. A Spanish translation of the terms of capitulation, bearing the date March 6, 1776, is in Special Collections, M. D. Anderson Library, University of Houston, Houston, Texas. For a brief description of this document, see Robert V. Haynes, "An Incident from the American Revolution," *Aldvs*, 12 (April, 1974), 2–6.

24. Phelps, *Memoirs and Adventures*, 110–12; Fitzpatrick to McGillivray, Struthers & Co, April 10, 1778, Letterbook of Fitzpatrick.

25. Chester to Germain, March 25, 1778, Anthony Hutchins to Lord Germain, May 21, 1778, English Provincial Records, VII, 348–49, 381–86.

26. Alexander Ross to John Stuart, March 5, 1778, Anonymous to John Campbell, March 1, 1778, Carleton Papers, nos. 989 and 968.

27. Entry of May 1, 1778, in Rowland, ed., *Life, Letters, and Papers of William Dunbar*, 60–61.

28. Starr, "Dons, Tories, and Rebels," 157, 159–60; Anonymous to John Campbell, March 1, 1778, Minutes of West Florida Council, March 18, 1778, Campbell to Stuart, n.d., Records of States, West Florida, series A, reel 8.

29. Entry of May 1, 1778, in Rowland, ed., *Life, Letters, and Papers of William Dunbar*, 61–62; Claiborne, *Mississippi*, 118–20.

30. Fitzpatrick to William Weir, August 12, 1778, Letterbook of Fitzpatrick. There is a hiatus in the letterbook of nearly two months duration, and the first letter after Willing's expedition was written from "Spanish Manchac."

31. Entry of May 1, 1778, in Rowland, ed., *Life, Letters and Papers of William Dunbar*, 63.

32. Testimony of Thomas Walters, March 2, 1778, Minutes of West Florida
Council, March 2, 1778, William Wilton to Governor Chester, March 8, 1778,
Minutes of West Florida Council, March 18, 1778, Records of States, West
Florida, series A, reel 8.
33. Memorial of Thomas McIntyre to Board of War, January 23, 1779, Pa-
pers of Continental Congress, item 41, VI, 101–103; Ford, ed., *Journals of the
Continental Congress*, XIII, 291–92; James Willing to Board of War, July 2, 1781,
Papers of Continental Congress, item 19, II, 223.
34. See for example, Claiborne, *Mississippi*, 117–23; Gayarré, *History of
Louisiana*, III, 109–14.
35. The most thorough defense of Willing's behavior is Caughey, "Willing's
Expedition Down the Mississippi," 5–36.
36. Entry of May 1, 1778, in Rowland, ed., *Life, Letters, and Papers of William
Dunbar*, 63. A note promising not to molest Dunbar and his property, signed
by James Willing and dated March 3, 1778, is in American Miscellaneous, Case
8, Box 20, Simon Gratz Autograph Collection, Historical Society of Pennsylvania.
37. Pollock to the President of Congress, September 18, 1782, Papers of the
Continental Congress, item 50. This particular letter is reprinted in toto as
Appendix 1 in James, *Oliver Pollock*, 347–55.
38. "A general diary of happenings and events in the Province of Louisiana
. . . ," n.d., Spanish Provincial Records, X, 122–24.
39. Hutchins to Germain, May 21, 1778, English Provincial Records, VII,
383–84.
40. Bernardo de Gálvez to José de Gálvez, March 11, 1778, quoted in
Caughey, "Willing's Expedition Down the Mississippi," 15; Richard McCarty
to John Askin, June 7, 1778, in Clarence W. Alvord, ed., *Kaskaskia Records,
1778–90*, Illinois State Historical Society, *Collections* (1915) X, 45; Chester to
Germain, April 14, 1778, English Provincial Records, VII, 365.
41. Oliver Pollock to Continental Congress, April 1, July 6, 1778, Papers of
Continental Congress, item 50.
42. Deposition of Alexander Ross, April 25, 1778, English Provincial Records, VII, 487.
43. Caughey, "Willing's Expedition Down the Mississippi," 13; Testimony
of Thomas Gibson, Minutes of West Florida Council, March 18, 1778, Records
of States, West Florida, series A, reel 8.
44. Chester to Germain, March 25, 1778, Petition, David Ross and Company,
English Merchants in the Mississippi, to Gálvez, April 11, 1778, English
Provincial Records, VII, 349, 445–46.
45. Chester to Gálvez, May 28, 1778, ibid., 516–18; Willing to Gálvez, March
24, 1778, Declaration of Stephen Shakespear, May 6, 1778, in Lawrence Kinnaird, ed., *Spain in the Mississippi Valley, 1765–94, Translation of Materials from
the Spanish Archives in the Bancroft Library*, American Historical Association,
Annual Report for the Year 1945 (Washington, D.C., 1949), II, pt. 1, pp. 260–61,
273–75.

168   NOTES

CHAPTER 4

1. Chester to Gálvez, May 28, 1778, Chester to Germain, March 25, 1778, English Provincial Records, VII, 517, 350.
2. Chester to Germain, March 25, 1778, ibid., 349–51.
3. Fergusson to Gálvez, March 14, 1778, ibid., 449–51; "A general diary of happenings," 125–26.
4. Fergusson to Gálvez, March 15, 1778, Gálvez to Fergusson, March 15, 20, and 21, 1778, English Provincial Records, VII, 451–54, 463–65, 471–72, 473.
5. Gálvez to Fergusson, March 18, 1778, ibid., 465–70; "A general diary of happenings," 124–25.
6. Willing to Gálvez, March 24, 1778, in Kinnaird, ed., *Spain in the Mississippi Valley*, pt. 1, pp. 260–61.
7. Fergusson to All His Britanick Majesty's Loyal Subjects in the Province of Louisiana and the Town of New Orleans, March 23, 1778, British Inhabitants to Captain Fergusson, March 27, 1778, Gálvez to Fergusson, April 1, 1778, Proclamation of Captain John Fergusson, April 3, 1778, English Provincial Records, VII, 477–79, 481–83, 474–75. Willing probably was referring to the three slaves Anthony Hutchins had surreptitiously taken from the guardhouse in New Orleans and placed on board the *Sylph*. See Hutchins to Germain, May 21, 1778, ibid., 382–83.
8. Gálvez to Chester, May 1, 1778, Deposition of Alexander Ross, April 25, 1778, ibid., 512–13, 489.
9. Chester to Germain, March 25, April 14, 1778, Extract from Minutes of the Council, April 25, 1778, ibid., 349–50, 369, 439; "A general diary of happenings," 125.
10. Deposition of William Ferguson, November 6, 1797, in Ellicott, *The Journal of Andrew Ellicott*, 130–32; Anthony Hutchins to Germain, May 21, 1778, Chester to Germain, May 7, 1778, English Provincial Records, VII, 383–88, 399–400; Willing to Committee on Congress, April 14, 1778, Papers of Continental Congress, item 78, XXIII, 494.
11. Chester to Germain, March 25, April 14, May 7, 1778, Extract of Minutes of Council, West Florida, May 21, 1778, English Provincial Records, VII, 351–52, 366–67, 393–94, 396–98. See also Wilbur H. Siebert, "The Loyalists in West Florida and the Natchez District," *Proceedings of the Mississippi Valley Historical Society*, 8 (1914–15), 108–10.
12. Willing to Committee of Congress, April 14, 1778, [Oliver Pollock] to Robert Morris et al., April 1, May 7, 1778, Papers of Continental Congress, item 78, XXIII, 494, 478, 480–81; Extract of Minutes of Council, West Florida, April 27, 1778, English Provincial Records, VII, 494–95; James A. Padgett, ed., "The Reply of Peter Chester, Governor of West Florida to Complaints Made Against His Administration," *Louisiana Historical Quarterly*, 22 (January, 1939), 43–44.
13. "A general diary of happenings," 126–31; Gálvez to Diego Joseph Navarro, April 14, 1778, in Kinnaird, ed., *Spain in the Mississippi Valley*, pt. 1, pp. 265–66.

14. "A general diary of happenings," 129; Nunn to Gálvez, April 14, 1778, Proclamation of Governor Gálvez, April 15, 1778, Gálvez to Nunn, April 21, 1778, English Provincial Records, VII, 441–44, 435, 417–18.

15. Nunn to Gálvez, April 16, 1778, Gálvez to Nunn, April 21, 1778, English Provincial Records, VII, 409–11, 417–18.

16. Gálvez to Nunn, April 19, 22, 1778, Nunn to Gálvez, April 23, May 1, 1778, ibid., 421, 423–24, 429–30, 431–32.

17. Kathryn T. Abbey, "Peter Chester's Defense of the Mississippi After the Willing Raid," Mississippi Valley Historical Review, 22 (June, 1935), 27–28; Hutchins to Germain, May 21, 1778, English Provincial Records, VII, 381–86.

18. Memorial of Robert Ross and John Campbell to Peter Chester and Council, September 9, 1778, Affidavit of Little Page Robertson, September 24, 1778, Depositions of Alexander Graiden, May 19 and 20, 1778, confession of Alexander Graiden, May 22, 1778, English Provincial Records, VIII, 25–35, 37–38, 110–14, 140–49. The sentences imposed by Gálvez are in ibid., 166–68.

19. Pollock to Commercial Committee of Congress, May 20, 1778, Papers of Continental Congress, item 78, XXIII.

20. Chester to Germain, June 2, 1778, John Osborne to Chester, July 4, 1778, Chester to Germain, August 24, 1778, English Provincial Records, VII, 507, 539–42, 534–35.

21. Claiborne, Mississippi, 123–24; Phelps, Memoirs and Adventures, 125–87; Brig. Genl. John Campbell to Sir Henry Clinton, April 7, 1779, in Great Britain, Historical Manuscripts Commission, Report on American Manuscripts in the Royal Institution of Great Britain (London, 1904–1907), I, 412.

22. Caughey, Bernardo de Gálvez in Louisiana, 127–28.

23. Willing to Pollock, May 30, 1778, in Kinnaird, ed., Spain in the Mississippi Valley, pt. 1, pp. 282–83.

24. Pollock to Commercial Committee, April 1, May 20, 1778, Papers of Continental Congress, item 50.

25. Pollock to Commercial Committee, July 6, 1778, Willing to Robert Morris et al., July 29, 1778, ibid., item 78, XXIII, 487.

26. Pollock to Commercial Committee, August 11, 1778, Pollock to President of Congress, September 18, 1782, ibid.; Journal of Joseph Bowman, entry of March 5, 1779, in James, ed., George Rogers Clark Papers, 164; Caughey, "Willing's Expedition Down the Mississippi," 33.

27. Robert George to Daniel Brodhead, September 25, 1779, Clark's Memoir, 1773–1779, in James, ed., George Rogers Clark Papers, 367–68, 298.

28. Willing to President of the Congress, May 12, 1779, Papers of the Continental Congress, item 78, XXIV, 29; Memorial of James Ellicot to Congress, n. d. [received January 2, 1779], ibid., item 41, III, 25; "Z" [Lewis J. Costigan] to George Washington, December 19, 1779, George Washington Papers, Library of Congress, XCIV, 111; Abraham Skinner to James Willing, September 4, 1781, Abraham Skinner Papers in Gratz Autograph Collection, Historical Society of Pennsylvania; "A Return of American Officers and Others, Prisoners on Long Island," August 15, 1778, in The Papers of Captain Rufus Lincoln of Wareham, Mass., comp. James Minor Lincoln (n. p., 1904), 32. Although the

last document bears the date August 15, 1778, the list includes prisoners taken in 1779. James Willing is listed as being taken "at sea," but no date is given for his capture.

29. Clark to Pollock, June 12, 1779, in James, ed., *George Rogers Clark Papers,* 330.

30. Clark to Fernando de Leyba, November 6, 1778, in Lawrence Kinnaird, ed., "Clark-Leyba Papers," *American Historical Review,* 41 (October, 1935), 101.

CHAPTER 5

1. Jacinto Panis to Gálvez, July 5, 1778, Spanish Provincial Records, X, 218–21. For a complete discussion of this mission, see John W. Caughey, "The Panis Mission to Pensacola, 1778," *Hispanic American Historical Review,* 10 (November, 1930), 480–89.

2. Entry of Sunday, December 13, 1778, in Rowland, ed., *Life, Letters, and Papers of William Dunbar,* 66.

3. Anonymous to Hutchins, May 11, 1778, Chester to Germain, September 19, 1778, English Provincial Records, VIII, 117–20, 175; Henry Atkins to Charles Stuart (copy), September 7, 1778, Chester to Germain, November 27, December 22, 1778, ibid., XVI, 60–61, 94, 125–126.

4. Chester to Germain, November 24, 1778, ibid., XVI, 65–70; Minutes of West Florida Council, April 27, June 6, June 20, September 10, October 1, 1778, Records of States, West Florida, series A, reel 8.

5. Minutes of the Lower House, October 1–8, 1778, October 15–November 4, 1778, Minutes of Upper House, October 7–8, October 15–November 5, 1778, Records of States, West Florida, series A, reel 3; Steill to Germain, October 15, 1778, English Provincial Records, VIII, 21–22; Starr, "Tories, Dons, and Rebels," 211–22.

6. Chester to Germain, November 24, 1778, Petition and Memorial of Speaker and Members of the Assembly of Province of West Florida to the King's Most Excellent Majesty in Council, November 25, 1778, Minutes of a Meeting of West Florida Merchants & Planters held at the Carolina Coffee House, March 10, 1779, English Provincial Records, VIII, 185–204, 243–54; Samuel Hannay to Germain, January 19, 1779, ibid., XVI, 4–5; Padgett, ed., "The Reply of Peter Chester," 31–46; Johnson, *British West Florida,* 213–14.

7. "Secret Instructions," King George III to Clinton, March 21, 1778, in Clinton Papers.

8. Clinton to Germain, October 8, 1778, ibid.; Ray Waldron Pettengill, trans., *Letters from America, 1776–1779; Being Letters of Brunswick, Hessian, and Waldeck Officers with the British Armies During the Revolution* (Port Washington, N.Y., 1964), 205; Max Von Eelking, *The German Allied Troops in the North American War of Independence, 1776–1783,* trans. J. G. Rosengarten (Albany, N.Y., 1893), 222.

9. Campbell to Germain, December 26, 1778, English Provincial Records, XVII, 1–2.

10. Campbell to Clinton, February 10, 1779, ibid., 12–14; Pettengill, trans., *Letters from America*, 226–27; Hugh Mackay Gordon to Edward Winslow, March 20, 1779, quoted in Starr, "Tories, Dons, and Rebels," 228.

11. Campbell to Clinton, February 10, 1779, English Provincial Records, XVII, 12–19. See also George C. Osborn, "Major-General John Campbell in British West Florida," *Florida Historical Quarterly*, 27 (April, 1949), 317–20.

12. Chester to Germain, November 27, 1778, English Provincial Records, XVI, 92–93; Campbell to Germain, April 7, 1779, ibid., XVII, 49; Minutes of West Florida Council, November 9, 1778, Records of States, West Florida, series A, reel 8.

13. Campbell to Germain, March 22, April 7, 1779, Germain to Campbell, June 24, 1779, English Provincial Records, XVII, 5–6, 49, 41–42.

14. This letter was received by General Clinton on July 28, 1779. A notation, apparently written by Clinton, reads: "It is meant [i.e. was it intended] that Sir Henry Clinton did not receive till July, '79, a copy of a letter to an officer acting under him, sent by Lord George Germain [in] July '78?" Henry Clinton, *The American Rebellion: Sir Henry Clinton's Narrative of His Campaigns: 1775–1782, with an Appendix of Original Documents*, ed. William B. Willcox (New Haven, 1954), 385 *n.*

15. Germain to General Officer Commanding in West Florida, July 1, 1778, Clinton Papers.

16. Ibid.; Starr, "Tories, Dons, and Rebels," 234; Osborn, "Major-General John Campbell in British West Florida," 318–19.

17. Campbell to Germain, March 22, 1779, Campbell to Clinton, February 10, English Provincial Records, XVII, 5–6, 14–19; Campbell to Clinton, March 25, 1779, Germain to Alexander Cameron and Thomas Browne, June 25, 1779, Carleton Papers, nos. 1856 and 2080.

18. Campbell to Clinton, March 10, May 10, 1779, Carleton Papers, nos. 1815 and 1989; Osborn, "Major-General John Campbell in British West Florida," 322–23.

19. Bernardo de Gálvez to José de Gálvez, July 3, 1779, Transcripts of Gálvez Letterbooks, Cuban Manuscripts, Box A, State Historical Society of Wisconsin, Madison; Caughey, *Bernardo de Gálvez in Louisiana*, 137–42.

20. Spain may have declared war as early as June 16, but the date generally given is June 21. Caughey, *Bernardo de Gálvez in Louisiana*, 149. On the confusion of dates see J. Horace Nunemaker, "Louisiana Anticipates Spain's Recognition of the Independence of the United States," *Louisiana Historical Quarterly*, 26 (July, 1943), 762.

21. Campbell to Clinton, September 11, 1779, Carleton Papers, no. 2281.

22. Gálvez to Navarro, October 16, 1779, Dispatches of the Governors of Louisiana to the Captains-General of Cuba, Spanish Archives, Box B, State Historical Society of Wisconsin; Gálvez to Navarro, August 17, 1779, Spanish Provincial Records, X, 300–302; Caughey, *Bernardo de Gálvez in Louisiana*, 149–51.

23. Bernardo de Gálvez to José de Gálvez, October 16, 1779, Spanish Provin-

172 NOTES

cial Records, X, 325–26; Gálvez to Navarro, August 19, 1779, Gálvez Letterbooks.

24. Bernardo de Gálvez to José de Gálvez, October 16, 1779, Spanish Provincial Records, X, 326–28; Campbell to Germain, September 14, 1779, English Provincial Records, XVII, 126.

25. Bernardo de Gálvez to José de Gálvez, October 16, 1779, Spanish Provincial Records, X, 328; Caughey, *Bernardo de Gálvez in Louisiana*, 153–54.

26. Campbell to Germain, September 14, 1779, English Provincial Records, XVII, 126–27; Campbell to Germain, December 15, 1779, ibid., XVIII, 72–74; Caughey, *Bernardo de Gálvez in Louisiana*, 154; Entry of [December] 22, 1779, in Rowland, ed., *Life, Letters, and Papers of William Dunbar*, 69–70.

27. Germain to Campbell, June 25, 1779, English Provincial Records, XVII, 89–90; Germain to Clinton, June 25, 1779, Clinton to Cornwallis, September 26, 1779, Clinton Papers; Starr, "Tories, Dons, and Rebels," 243–46.

28. Campbell to Clinton, September 11, 1779, Carleton Papers, no. 2281; Dickson to Gálvez, March 27, April 26, 1779, Spanish Provincial Records, X, 285, 287.

29. Campbell to Chester, September 9, 10, 1779, James Campbell to Captain Le Montais, September 10, 1779, Carleton Papers, nos. 2267, 2277, 2275; Minutes of West Florida Council, September 10, 11, 1779, Records of States, West Florida, series A, reel 8; Chester to Germain, November 15, 1779, English Provincial Records, VIII, 364.

30. Campbell to Germain, September 14, 1779, English Provincial Records, XVII, 127; Dickson to Gálvez, March 5, 1779, Francisco Collel to Gálvez, March 15, July 5, 1779, Spanish Provincial Records, X, 283, 245, 259–60.

31. Dickson to Campbell, March 12, 13, 1779, Campbell to Germain, April 7, 1779 with enclosures: Report of Francis Miller and Report of J. J. Graham, English Provincial Records, XVII, 48–62.

32. Dickson to Campbell, March 13, 1779, Campbell to Germain, April 7, September 14, 1779, ibid., 62, 50–52, 126.

33. Extract of letter Captain Alexander McIntosh to Chester, October 16, 1778, Chester to Germain, November 27, 1778, ibid., XVI, 92–93, 95–96. See entry of April and May, 1779 in Rowland, ed., *Life, Letters, and Papers of William Dunbar*, 68–70.

34. Extract from Journal of Lt. Col. Dickson, entry of September 22, 1779, Campbell to Germain, September 14, 1779, English Provincial Records, XVII, 84–85, 126–27; Collel to Gálvez, August 31, 1779, Spanish Provincial Records, X, 269–70. Dickson apparently learned of the attack from an American who was caught drawing a plan of the fort at Manchac. See Collel to Gálvez, ibid., 263.

35. Gálvez to Navarro, September 18, 1779, Dispatches of Governors of Louisiana; Bernardo de Gálvez to José de Gálvez, October 16, 1779, Spanish Provincial Records, X, 329. On the casualties at Manchac, see Henry P. Dent, ed., "West Florida: the Capture of Baton Rouge by Gálvez, September 21st, 1779," *Louisiana Historical Quarterly*, 12 (April, 1929), 265.

36. Bernardo de Gálvez to José de Gálvez, October 16, 1779, Spanish Provin-

NOTES 173

cial Records, X, 329; Campbell to Germain, September 14, 1779, English
Provincial Records, XVII, 129.

37. Gálvez to Navarro, September 18, 1779, Dispatches of Governor of
Louisiana; Gálvez to José de Gálvez, October 16, 1779, Spanish Provincial
Records, X, 329–30; Caughey, *Bernardo de Gálvez in Louisiana*, 155–57.

38. Gálvez to José de Gálvez, October 16, 1779, Spanish Provincial Records,
X, 330; Lt. Col. Dickson's reasons for removing to Baton Rouge, September
22, 1779, Articles of Capitulation, September 21, 1779, in Dent, ed., "Capture
of Baton Rouge," 258–64; Albert W. Haarman, "The Spanish Conquest of
British West Florida," *Florida Historical Quarterly* 39 (October, 1960), 111–13.

39. Gálvez to José de Gálvez, October 16, 1779, Spanish Provincial Records,
X, 331; Oliver Pollock to the Inhabitants of the Natchez, September 8, 1779,
quoted in Jack D. L. Holmes, "Juan de la Villebeuvre: Spain's Commandant
of Natchez During the American Revolution," *Journal of Mississippi History*,
37 (February, 1975), 113–14; Pollock to the Inhabitants of the Natchez district,
September 23, 1779, Archivo General de Indias (Sevilla) Papeles procedentes
de la Isla de Cuba, legajo 192. The author wishes to thank Douglas Inglis for
sharing the results of his research in Spanish sources with him.

40. Pickles to Piernas, September 14, 1779, quoted in Caughey, *Bernardo de
Gálvez in Louisiana*, 159–60; Gerard Brandon et al. to [Pollock], October 16,
1779, quoted in Claiborne, *Mississippi*, 122 n.

41. Isaac Johnson to Anthony Hutchins, October 5, 1779, copy in Minutes
of West Florida Council, October 25, 1779, Nehemiah Carter to Hutchins,
October 6, 1779, Dr. Edward Dwight to Hutchins, October 6, 1779, Records
of States, West Florida, series A, reel 8.

42. Johnson to Hutchins, October 5, 1779, ibid.; Address of the Inhabitants
of Natchez to Lt. Col. Dickson, October 4, 1779, printed in Kenneth Scott,
ed., "Britain Loses Natchez, 1779: An Unpublished Letter," *Journal of Mississippi History*, 26 (February 1964), 45–46.

43. Minutes of West Florida Council, October 25, 1779, Records of States,
West Florida, series A, reel 8.

44. Caughey, *Bernardo de Gálvez in Louisiana*, 162; Martin de Mayorca to José
de Gálvez, October 4, 1780, in Kinnaird, ed., *Spain in Mississippi Valley*, II, pt.
2, p. 386.

45. Return of Prisoners and Killed and Wounded, in Dent, ed., "Capture of
Baton Rouge," 264–65; Gálvez to José de Gálvez, October 16, 1779, Spanish
Provincial Records, X, 331; Campbell to Germain, December 15, 1779, English
Provincial Records, XVII, 74–80.

46. Gálvez to Navarro, October 16, 1779, Spanish Provincial Records, X,
315–17; Gálvez to Navarro, December 2, 1779, Gálvez Letterbooks; Campbell
to Germain, December 15, 1779, English Provincial Records, XVII, 74–77;
Campbell to Clinton, February 12, 1780, Carleton Papers, no. 2570.

47. The campaign from the Spanish point of view can be followed in "Diary
kept by Don Bernardo de Gálvez, Brigadier of the Royal Writers, Governor
of the Province of Louisiana, in charge of His Majesty's expedition against
Pensacola and Mobile," March 18, 1780, Spanish Provincial Records, X,

174

345–48; Chester to Tonyn, February 18, 1780, Carleton Papers, no. 2583.
48. "Diary of Gálvez," 349–52; Caughey, *Bernardo de Gálvez in Louisiana,* 176–77.
49. Gálvez to Durnford, March 1, 1780, Carleton Papers, no. 2601; Durnford to Campbell, March 2, 1780, English Provincial Records, XVII, 108–109; "Diary of Gálvez," 352–59.
50. Campbell to Germain, March 24, 1780, English Provincial Records, XVII, 103–105.
51. "Diary of Gálvez," 360–64; Caughey, *Bernardo de Gálvez in Louisiana,* 180–81.
52. Durnford to Campbell, March 14, 1780, Articles of Capitulation proposed by Elias Durnford, March 13, 1780, English Provincial Records, XVII, 110, 112–16; Articles of Capitulation, March 13, 1780, in Carleton Papers, no. 2636; Gálvez to [Navarro], March 20, 1780, Spanish Provincial Records, X, 364–66; Caughey, *Bernardo de Gálvez in Louisiana,* 182–85, 214.

CHAPTER 6

1. Bernardo Gálvez to José de Gálvez, n.d., Spanish Provincial Records, X, 390–96; Campbell to Germain, May 15, November 26, 1780, January 5, 1781, Campbell to Parker, May 13, 1780, English Provincial Records, XVII, 132–33, 200–202, 204; Caughey, *Bernardo de Gálvez in Louisiana,* 191–93; O'Donnell, *Southern Indians,* 99–102, Campbell to Clinton, March 28, 1780, Clinton Papers; Osborne, "Major-General John Campbell in British West Florida," 331–36.
2. Campbell to Germain, January 5, 1781, English Provincial Records, XVII, 202–204; Haarmann, "The Spanish Conquest of British West Florida," 120; Starr, "Tories, Dons, and Rebels," 308.
3. Campbell to Germain, January 7, 11, 1781, English Provincial Records, XVII, 204–206; Campbell to Clinton, January 7, February 15, 1781, Carleton Papers, nos. 9900 and 9901; Saavedra to José de Gálvez, February 16, 1781, quoted in Caughey, *Bernardo de Gálvez in Louisiana,* 195; Eelking, *German Allied Troops,* 223.
4. The best contemporary account of the siege of Pensacola is the diary of Governor-General Bernardo de Gálvez in Spanish Provincial Records, X, 345–64. See also the translation by Gaspar Cusachs of the diary as later published in Bernardo de Gálvez, "Diary of the Operations Against Pensacola," *Louisiana Historical Quarterly,* 1 (January, 1917), 46–75. A more accurate translation of the same is in Orwin N. Rush, *The Battle of Pensacola* (Tallahassee, 1966), 41–84. The English side is more briefly described in Robert Farmar's "A Journal of the Siege of Pensacola . . . ," Florida Papers, Miscellaneous, 1525–1821, Library of Congress. A copy of the journal appears in James A. Padgett, ed., "Bernardo de Gálvez's Siege of Pensacola in 1781 (As Related in Robert Farmar's Journal)," *Louisiana Historical Quarterly,* 26 (April, 1943), 311–27. See also Campbell to Clinton, April 9, 1781, Carleton Papers, no. 9913;

Campbell to Germain, May 7, 1781, English Provincial Records, XVII, 217–20.

5. Campbell to Germain, May 12, 1781, English Provincial Records, XVIII, 220–25; Campbell to Clinton, May 12, 1781, Carleton Papers, no. 9918. The negotiations between Gálvez and Campbell can be followed in English Provincial Records, XVIII, 235–38. The Articles of Capitulation are in Rush, *The Battle of Pensacola,* 84–91.

6. This chapter follows closely the interpretation offered by John W. Caughey in "The Natchez Rebellion of 1781 and Its Aftermath," *Louisiana Historical Quarterly,* 16 (January, 1933), 57–83. See also Holmes, "Juan de la Villebeuvre," 104–105; Gibson, *The Chickasaws,* 72–73.

7. Campbell to Clinton, July 27, 1781, Carleton Papers, no. 9925; Starr, "Tories, Dons, and Rebels," 358–59; Testimony of Mayo Gray, May 9, 1781, Spanish Provincial Records, X, 428–29. A copy of John Blommart's commission is in Kinnaird, ed., *Spain in Mississippi Valley,* pt. 1, p. 424.

8. Caughey, "Natchez Rebellion of 1781," 58–59; Claiborne, *Mississippi,* 127.

9. Hutchins to [Miró], July 10, 1785, AGI, PC, 198; Campbell to Clinton, July 27, 1781, Carleton Papers, no. 9925; Testimony of Mayo Gray, May 9, 1781, Spanish Provincial Records, X, 428–29.

10. Holmes, "Juan de la Villebeuvre," 108; Caughey, "Natchez Rebellion of 1781," 59; Campbell to Clinton, July 27, 1781, Carleton Papers, no. 9925.

11. Juan de la Villebeuvre, "Journal de cequi cest passé du depuis le 21 du Mois D'Avril 1781 jusqu'a mon arrivée á la Nuc Orleans," AGI, PC, leg. 194; Anderson, ed., "Narrative of John Hutchins," 7.

12. Caughey, "Natchez Rebellion of 1781," 60; Holmes, "Juan de la Villebeuvre," 109; Miró to Diego Joseph Navarro, May 25, 1781, copy in Dispatches of the Governor of Louisiana to the Captains-General of Cuba, Spanish Archives, Box B, Wisconsin Historical Society, Madison, Wisc.

13. Caughey, "Natchez Rebellion of 1781," 60.

14. Testimony of Mayo Gray, May 9, 1781, Miró to Gálvez, June 6, 1781, Spanish Provincial Records, X, 425–26, 432–33.

15. Miró to Navarro, May 25, 1781, Dispatches of Governor of Louisiana, Box B; Miró to Gálvez, June 6, 1781, Spanish Provincial Records, X, 424–26.

16. Caughey, "Natchez Rebellion of 1781," 62–63.

17. The correspondence between Campbell and Gálvez on these matters is in Carleton Papers, no. 9922. See also Campbell to Clinton, May 31, July 17, 1781, ibid., nos. 9920 and 9925.

18. Caughey, "Natchez Rebellion of 1781," 63–65.

19. Anderson, ed., "Narrative of John Hutchins," 7–8; declaration of Don Silbestre Labadie, July 5, 1782, in Kinnaird, ed., *Spain in Mississippi Valley,* pt. 2, p. 29. In early February of 1782, Pedro Piernas, Lieutenant Governor of Louisiana, reported that the Indians had killed Hutchins. Piernas to Gálvez, February 6, 1782, AGI, PC, 1377.

20. Claiborne, *Mississippi,* 129–32; Grand-Pré to Miró, May 26, 1782, in Kinnaird, ed., *Spain in Mississippi Valley,* pt. 2, pp. 16–17; John Holston to Stephen Holston & Judith, his wife, May 15, 1782, in Louis Houck, ed., *The Spanish*

176   NOTES

Regime in Missouri (Chicago, 1909), I, 220–21; Caughey, "Natchez Rebellion of 1781," 68; Grand-Pré to Piernas, November 20, 1781, AGI, PC, 1376.
21. Draft of Gálvez to _____, June 16, 1781, quoted in Caughey, "Natchez Rebellion of 1781," 65.
22. Sale of Property Belonging to English Prisoners, May 6, 1782, in Kinnaird, ed., *Spain in Mississippi Valley*, pt. 2, pp. 12–13; Etats de efe que nous avons perda aux nache par ordre de Mᶜ Bloumart et antre office de la revotte. July 28, 1781, AGI, PC 193¹³; Ymbentario, estima.ᵒⁿ Venta y remittes de 15 negros de diferentes sexos y edades procedentes de Juan Blomar y otros Capitanes de la rebelion del puesto de Natches. Año de 1782. AGI, PC, 684; Resultat des ventes publique des Biens des rebelles fugitifs et autres dans Les prisons de La Nᵉˡˡᵉ Orleans, Les droits du Juge, Alquarilo, Interprettes, Engagés, et payments óu remises faile à Davens Conforment aux pieces Justificatives Anéxées aux Minuttes, soustraits and enclousee, May 6, 1782. AGI, PC, 193ᴬ; Relacion du Produit des ventes des habitantes, faites par Le Luietenant Colonel Gradúe,ᵭ Carlos de Grand Pré, Procédant des Saises Et. Confiscations Sur Les Rebelles fugitives du district des Natchez, Les quelles dittes Sommes, Liquides, il Remêt a Monsuier Le Colonelᵭ Estevan Miró,—Governeur Genl. Interin de Citte Province de La Louisiane Ec, Oct. 11, 1782, AGI, PC, 193ᴬ; and Relacion de los que Deven las Almanedes de los bienes de los Rebeldes fugitivos, Oct. 11, 1782, AGI, PC, 193ᴬ.
23. Archibald Campbell to Gálvez, November 29, 1781, in Kinnaird, *Spain in Mississippi Valley*, pt. 1, pp. 435–36; Bethune to Commandant at Natchez, July 19, 1781, quoted in Caughey, "Natchez Rebellion of 1781," 69.
24. Adair, *The History of the American Indians*, 370; Gibson, *Chickasaws*, 65; Declaration of Labadie, July 5, 1782, in Kinnaird, ed., *Spain in Mississippi Valley*, pt. 2, p. 31.
25. Miró to Cagigal, May 4, 1782, Dispatches of Governors of Louisiana, Box B. See also Miró to Gálvez, May 4, 1782, in Houck, ed., *Spanish Regime in Missouri*, I, 213.
26. Declaration of Labadie, July 5, 1782, in Kinnaird, ed., *Spain in Mississippi Valley*, pt. 2, pp. 24–25.
27. Declaration of Madame Cruzat, May 30, 1782, in Houck, ed., *Spanish Regime in Missouri*, I, 221–31; Declaration of Labadie, July 5, 1782, in Kinnaird, ed., *Spain in Mississippi Valley*, pt. 2, pp. 25–26.
28. Declaration of Labadie, July 5, 1782, in Kinnaird, ed., *Spain in Mississippi Valley*, pt. 2, pp. 26–27, 29, 32; "Palava de Honor," May 15, 1782, AGI, PC, 1826 and 2359.
29. Colbert to [Governor of Louisiana], May 15, 1782, declaration of Madame Cruzat, May 30, 1782, AGI, PC, 1826, 2359, and Santo Domingo, 2656; Declaration of Labadie, July 5, 1782, in Kinnaird, ed., *Spain in Mississippi Valley*, pt. 2, pp. 33–34.
30. Navarro to Gálvez, June 4, 1782, in Kinnaird, ed., *Spain in Mississippi Valley*, pt. 2, pp. 18–19; Grand-Pré to Miró, May 26, 1782, no. 246, AGI, PC, 9ª; Miró tò Gálvez, June 5, 1782, no. 12, AGI, SD, 2656.
31. Miró to Gálvez, June 5, 1782, no. 12, AGI, SD, 2656; Miró to Cagigal,

July 6, 1782, no. 29, AGI, PC, 1304; Caughey, "Natchez Rebellion of 1781," 75–77; Colbert to Miró, October 6, 1782, in Kinnaird, ed., *Spain in Mississippi Valley*, pt. 2, p. 60.

32. Cruzat to Miró, August 8, 1782, Henrique Grimarest, Report on the Mission of Paulous to the Chickasaws [September, 1782], Spanish Overtures to the Chickasaws, October 24, 1782, Pedro Piernas to Miró, October 28, 1782, in Kinnaird, ed., *Spain in Mississippi Valley*, pt. 2, pp. 50–52, 57–58, 61–63.

33. Cruzat to Miró, August 8, 1782, ibid., 51–54.

34. Gibson, *Chickasaws*, 74–76.

35. Gálvez to Prince William, Duke of Lancaster, April 6, 1783, [Prince] William Henry to Galvez, April 13, 1783, AGI, Indiferente General, 1578; Caughey, "Natchez Rebellion of 1781," 81; Jos Rowley to Governor of Louisiana, April 19, 1783, AGI, PC, 196; Parole of Natchez Rebels, April 28, 1783, ibid.

36. Caughey, "Natchez Rebellion of 1781," 81–82.

37. Du Breuil to Miró, November 8, 1783, in Kinnaird, ed., *Spain in Mississippi Valley*, pt. 2, pp. 90–91.

CHAPTER 7

1. Starr, "Tories, Dons, and Rebels," 362–64.

2. A. Z. to Lord Thurlow, October 9, 1782, Earl of Shelburne Papers, W. L. Clements Library.

3. Jack D. L. Holmes, "Robert Ross: Plan for an English Invasion of Louisiana in 1782," *Louisiana History*, 5 (Spring, 1964), 161–77; J. Leitch Wright, Jr., "Lord Dunmore's Loyalist Asylum in the Floridas," *Florida Historical Quarterly*, 49 (April, 1971), 370–79.

4. Samuel Flagg Bemis, *The Diplomacy of the American Revolution* (Bloomington, Ind., 1957), 228–64.

Essay on Sources

This study depends heavily upon primary sources located in the Mississippi Department of Archives and History at Jackson. The British side of the American Revolution in the old Southwest can be followed in the English Provincial Records which consist of handwritten transcripts of documents from the Public Records Office in London and are primarily from the Colonial Office, 5th series (America and the West Indies), volumes 582–597. Less complete but still somewhat helpful are the Spanish Provincial Records which consist of handwritten transcripts of documents from the Papeles procedentes de la Isla de Cuba in the Archivo General de Indias at Seville, Spain.

The military aspects of the Revolution in and around the Natchez District may be gleaned from the Sir Guy Carleton (British Headquarters) Papers available in photostatic form at Colonial Williamsburg Foundation. The originals are in the British Public Records Office (P.R.O. 30/55) in London. This collection is calendared in "Report on American Manuscripts in the Royal Institution of Great Britain," *Historical Manuscripts Commission*, 4 vols. (London, Dublin, and Hereford, 1904–1909). The Sir Henry Clinton Papers at the William L. Clements Library on the campus of the University of Michigan at Ann Arbor also proved extremely useful. Manuscript sources on the Willing Raid are surprisingly scarce. The voluminous papers of the Continental Congress, especially the Oliver Pollock Papers (item 50) and Letters Addressed to Congress (item 78), were invaluable in ascertaining the American objectives.

Equally helpful were microfilms of the legislative proceedings of British West Florida in the Records of the States of the United States of America. For a complete listing of these records, see *A Guide to the Microfilm Collection of Early State Records*, Lillian A. Hamrick, ed., and William S. Jenkins, comp. (Washington, D.C., 1950) and *The Supplement*, William S. Jenkins, ed. (Washington, D.C., 1951). Less useful were the Oliver Pollock Papers in the Library of Congress, the General Edward Hand and Abraham Skinner Papers in the Gratz Autograph Collection in the Historical Society of Pennsylvania, and the George Rogers Clark Papers in the Lyman Draper Collection in the State Historical Society of Wisconsin at Madison.

The Spanish records are not only the most extensive but also the most inaccessible to American scholars. An indication of the magnitude of these records may be gained from Roscoe R. Hill, *Descriptive Catalogue of the Documents Relating to the History of the United States in the Papeles Procedentes de Cuba deposited in the Archivo General de Indias at Seville* (Washington, D.C., 1916). In addition to the transcripts in the Mississippi Department of Archives and History, the Louis Houck Collection in the State Historical Society of Wisconsin contains the Dispatches of the Governors of Louisiana to the Captains-General of Cuba and the letterbooks of Governor Bernardo de Gálvez. Douglas Inglis, a graduate student at Texas Christian University, kindly permitted me to examine the notes he had taken from Spanish documents in the Archivo General de Indias and the microfilm copies of records pertaining to early Natchez in his possession.

Additional information, primarily about the social and economic life of the Old Natchez District, may be found in the Letterbooks of John Fitzpatrick in the New York Public Library, the Thomas Gage and Earl of Shelburne Papers in the William L. Clements Library, and the William Dunbar Papers in the Mississippi Department of Archives and History. An interesting letter, written by Michael Martyn and bearing the date August 17, 1774, is in the Mississippi Department of Archives and History.

Contemporary descriptions of the area provide much useful information. These include Bernard Romans, *A Concise Natural History of East and West Florida* (Gainesville, Florida, 1962); Thomas Hutchins, *An Historical Narrative and Topographical Description of Louisiana and West Florida* (Philadelphia, 1784); Philip Pittman, *The Present State of European Settlements on the Mississippi* (London, 1770); and William Bartram, *Travels of William Bartram*, Mark van Doren, ed. (New York, 1928). A classic study of the southern Indians is James Adair, *The History of the American Indians, Particularly of the Nations Adjoining the Mississippi, East and West Florida, Georgia, South and North Carolina, and Virginia* (London, 1775). Additional information is in W. M. Carpenter, ed., "The Mississippi River in the Olden Time: A Genuine Account of the Present State of the River Mississippi and of the Land on its Banks to the River Yasous, 1776," *De Bow's Review*, 3 (1847), 115–23; John H. Wynne, *General History of the British Empire in America; Containing an Historical, Political, and Commercial View of the English Settlements; Including All the Countries in North America, and the West Indies, Ceded by the Peace of Paris*, 2 vols. (London, 1770); Benjamin L. C. Wailes, *Report on the Agriculture and Geology of Mississippi, Embracing a Sketch of the Social and Natural History of the State* (Philadelphia, 1854); and Francis Bouligny, "Memoirs on Louisiana in 1776," in Alcée Fortier, *A History of Louisiana*, 4 vols. (New York, 1904), II, 25–57. Two other contemporary accounts deserve special mention. The diary of William Dunbar offers the best description of the daily life of an early planter. Although poorly edited by Eron O. Rowland, the diary is available in published form in *Life, Letters and Papers of William Dunbar* (Jackson, 1930). The trials and tribulations of a less successful settler are recounted in Matthew Phelps, *Memoirs and Adventures of Captain Matthew Phelps, formerly of Harwington in Connecticut, now Resident in Newhaven in Vermont, Particularly in Two Voyages from Connecticut to the River Mississippi, from December 1773 to October 1780 . . .* , Anthony Haswell, comp. (Bennington, Vt., 1802).

Most of the official records pertaining to the American Revolution in the old Southwest are still unpublished, but there are a few exceptions. Dunbar Rowland, while he was director of the Mississippi Department of Archives and History, planned to publish the English Provincial Records, but he brought out only one volume—*Mississippi Provincial Archives, 1763–1766, English Dominion* (Nashville, Tenn., 1911). His wife, Eron O. Rowland, edited part of the correspondence of Governor Peter Chester which appeared as "Peter Chester, Third Governor of the Province of West Florida under British Dominion, 1770–1781," *Publications of the Mississippi Historical Society*, Centenary Series (Jackson, 1925), V, 1–183. Far more valuable are two sets of published Spanish sources—Louis Houck, ed., *The Spanish Regime in Missouri*, 2 vols. (Chicago, 1909) and Lawrence Kinnaird, ed., *Spain in the Mississippi Valley, 1765–1794, Translation of materials from the Spanish Archives in the Bancroft Library, American Historical Association, Annual Report for the Year 1945* (Washington, 1949), II, parts 1–3. Also helpful are James A. Robertson, ed., "Spanish Correspondence Concerning the American Revolution," *Hispanic American Historical Review*, 1 (August, 1918), 299–316 and Lawrence Kinnaird, ed., "Clark-Leyba Papers," *American Historical Review*, 41 (October, 1935), 92–112.

Other printed sources include Clarence E. Carter, ed., *The Correspondence of General Thomas Gage with the Secretary of State, 1763–1775*, 2 vols. (New Haven, 1931–33); James Wilkinson, *Memoirs of Own Times*, 2 vols. (Philadelphia, 1816); Washington C. Ford, et al., eds., *Journals of the Continental Congress*, 34 vols. (Washington, D.C., 1921–1936); Reuben Gold Thwaites and Louise Phelps Kellogg, eds., *Frontier Defense on the Upper Ohio* (Madison, Wisc., 1912); James A. James, ed., *George Rogers Clark Papers, 1771–1781*, Illinois State Historical Library, *Collections* (1912), VIII; John Q. Anderson, ed., "The Narrative of John Hutchins," *Journal of Mississippi History*, 20 (January, 1958), 1–29; Clarence W. Alvord, ed., *Kaskaskia Records, 1778–90*, Illinois State Historical Library, *Collections* (1915), X; James A. Padgett, ed., "The Reply of Governor Peter Chester, Governor of West Florida, to Complaints Made Against His Administration," *Louisiana Historical Quarterly*, 22 (January 1939), 31–46; James Minor Lincoln, comp., *The Papers of Captain Rufus Lincoln of Wareham, Mass.* (n. p., 1904); Ray Waldron Pettengill, trans., *Letters from America, 1776–1779; Being Letters of Brunswick, Hessian, and Waldeck Officers with the British Armies During the Revolution* (Port Washington, N. Y., 1964); William B. Willcox, ed., *The American Rebellion: Sir Henry Clinton's Narrative of His Campaigns: 1775–1782, with an Appendix of Original Documents* (New Haven, 1965); Henry P. Dent, ed., "West Florida: The Capture of Baton Rouge by Gálvez, September 21st, 1779," *Louisiana Historical Quarterly*, 12 (April, 1929), 255–66; Kenneth Scott, ed., "Britain Loses Natchez, 1779: An Unpublished Letter," *Journal of Mississippi History*, 26 (February, 1964), 45–46; James A. Padgett, ed., "Bernardo de Gálvez's Siege of Pensacola in 1781 (As Related in Robert Farmar's Journal)," *Louisiana Historical Quarterly*, 26 (April, 1943); 311–327.

Although the American Revolution in the Old Southwest has been largely neglected by historians, there are a few valuable secondary accounts. For background information, Cecil Johnson's *British West Florida, 1763–1783* (New Haven, 1942) is invaluable. Clayton James' *Antebellum Natchez* (Baton Rouge, 1968) contains a good general description of the early years of the district. Clinton Howard's *The British Development of West Florida, 1763–1769* (Berkeley, Calif., 1947) is less complete, but the appendix includes a listing of the early land grants. See also Moreau B. C. Chambers, "History of Fort Panmure at Natchez, 1763–1785" (M.A. thesis, Duke University, 1942); Cecil Johnson, "The Distribution of Land in British West Florida," *Louisiana Historical Quarterly*, 16 (October 1933): 639–53; and two articles by Clinton Howard: "Colonial Natchez: the Early British Period," *Journal of Mississippi History*, 7 (July 1945), 156–86 and "Some Economic Aspects of British West Florida, 1763–1768," *Journal of Southern History*, 6 (May 1940), 201–21.

The most complete account of British West Florida during the American Revolution is Joseph Barton Starr, "Tories, Dons, and Rebels: The American Revolution in British West Florida" (Ph.D. dissertation, Florida State University, 1971). The Spanish side of the story is ably covered in John Walton Caughey, *Bernardo de Gálvez in Louisiana, 1776–1783* (Berkeley, Calif., 1934). Other useful studies include Clarence W. Alvord, *The Mississippi Valley in British Politics: A Study of the Trade, Land Speculation and Experiments in Imperialism Culminating in the American Revolution*, 2 vols. (New York, 1959); John W. Caughey, "Bernardo de Gálvez and the English Smugglers on the Mississippi, 1777," *Hispanic American Historical Review*, 12 (February, 1932), 46–58; Kathryn T. Abbey, "Peter Chester's Defense of the Mississippi After the Willing Raid," *Mississippi Valley Historical Review*, 22 (June, 1935), 17–32; Albert W. Haarmann, "The Spanish Conquest of British West Florida, 1779–1781," *Florida Historical Quarterly*, 31 (October, 1960), 107–34; Philip M. Hamer, "John Stuart's Indian Policy during the Early Months of the American Revolution," *Mississippi Valley Historical Review*, 17 (December, 1930), 351–66; James A. James, "Spanish Influence in the West during the American Revolution," *Mississippi Valley Historical Review*, 4 (December, 1917), 193–208; George C. Osborn, "Major-General John Campbell in British West Florida," *Florida Historical Quarterly*, 27 (April, 1949), 317–39; N. Orwin Rush, *Spain's Final Triumph Over Great Britain in the Gulf of Mexico: The Battle of Pensacola, March 29 to May 8, 1781* (Tallahassee, 1966); Wilbur H. Seibert, "Loyalists in West Florida and the Natchez District," *Mississippi Valley Historical Review*, 2 (March, 1916), 465–83.

The activities of the Waldeck Regiments in the campaigns of West Florida may be followed in Max von Eelking, *The German Allied Troops in the North American War of Independence*, trans. and abridged by J. D. Rosengarten (Albany, 1893). The work of George Morgan and Oliver Pollock is covered in Max Savelle, *George Morgan: Colony Builder* (New York, 1967) and James Alton James, *Oliver Pollock: The Life and Times of an Unknown Patriot* (New York and London, 1937). On British Indian policy see John Alden, *John Stuart and the Southern Frontier* (Ann Arbor, 1944); James H. O'Donnell, III, *Southern Indians in the American Revolution* (Knoxville, 1973); and Arrell M. Gibson, *The Chickasaws* (Norman, Okla, 1971). Several older and general histories of the region contain valuable information although they must be used with caution. The most useful are Charles Gayarré, *The History of Louisiana*, 4 vols. (New Orleans, 1930); François-Xavier Martin, *The History of Louisiana from the Earliest Period* (New Orleans, 1882); J. F. H. Claiborne, *Mississippi as a Province, Territory, and State* (Jackson, 1880); Peter Joseph Hamilton, *Colonial Mobile* (Mobile, 1952).

Index

Alexander, Harry, 68.
Alston, John, 135, 137, 142.
Alston, Philip, 135, 137, 143.
Amite River, 23, 84, 117.
Arkansas Post, 24, 37.
Arnold, Benedict, 53.
Atalanta, British frigate, 43–44, 46.
Attakapas (La.), 24.
A.Z. (loyalist pseudonym), 154, 155.

Baird, James, 31.
Bartram, William, English botanist, 22, 23.
Bassett, Thomas, 31.
Baton Rouge (La.): early history of, 20; attacked by James Willing, 67; results of Willing's raid, 68–69; Spanish campaign against, 120–122; feelings toward Spanish, 124.
Bay, Elisha Hall, 83.
Bethune, Farquhar, 65, 114, 143, 153–154.
Bingamin, Samuel, 140.
Blommart, John: Natchez merchant, 12; former British officer, 19; participant in Natchez Rebellion, 135–138; surrenders to Spaniards, 140; property confiscated, 143; freed by Spaniards, 147, 151.
Board of Trade (London), 11.
Board of War (Continental Congress), 53.
Bradley, John, 12.

Browne, Montfort, Lieutenant Governor and Acting Governor of West Florida, 7, 20.
Buckler, Christian, 32.
Burdon, George, Lieutenant, 42, 78.
Byrd, Thomas Taylor, 31.

Calvert, Joseph, 74.
Cameron, Alexander, 109.
Campbell, Archibald, Governor of Jamaica, 143.
Campbell, David, 83.
Campbell, John, British merchant, 91–92.
Campbell, John, Brigadier General: assumes command of British troops in West Florida, 105–106; arrives in Pensacola, 106–107; rebuilds western fortifications, 108–110, 115–117; apprehensive about Spanish invasion, 127; attempts to relieve Mobile, 129–130; orders attack on Mobile Village, 132; in Pensacola campaign, 132–133; encourages Natchez rebellion, 134–135; denies involvement in Natchez rebellion, 139.
Carolina Coffee House (Pensacola), 105.
Carpenter, Caleb, merchant: describes Natchez District, 8–9.
Carradine, Parker, 143, 148.
Carteret, packet boat, 116.

Eliot, James, 66, 98.
Ellis, Richard, 65.

Fairchild, Henry, 12.
Farmer, Robert, Major, 6.
Farrell, Dr. Francis, 139.
Ferguson, William, 85–86.
Fergusson, John, Captain: commander of *Sylph*, 78; dispatched to New Orleans, 78–83; comes to rescue of *Catherine*, 93.
Fitzpatrick, John, 22, 37, 66, 69, 92.
Flowers, Samuel, 21.
Forbes, William, Major, 5–6.
Forster, Anthony, Captain, 95, 124–125.
Fort Bute, 21, 84, 88, 108, 119.
Fort Carlos III, 147, 151.
Fort Charlotte: Spanish attack on, 129–130; mentioned, 127, 128, 132.
Fort George, 131, 132, 133.
Fort Panmure: captured by Willing, 64; repaired by British, 88, 94; surrendered to Spaniards, 121–122; occupied by Spanish troops, 124–125; during Natchez rebellion, 135–140; Spanish policy toward, 147; mentioned, 11, 19, 118, 139, 153.
Fort Pitt, 33, 35, 51, 53, 58, 59, 91.
Fort Rosalie, 3–4, 11.
French: settle in Natchez, 3; in Louisiana Province, 23; involved in rebellion, 34.

Gage, Thomas, General, 28.
Gálvez, Bernardo de, Governor of Louisiana: takes census of New Orleans, 24; policy toward British shipping, 40–42; negotiations with Captain Thomas Lloyd, 43–47; encourages French trade, 47; correspondence with George Morgan, 51–53; welcomes James Willing in New Orleans, 72–73; negotiations with Captain Fergusson, 79–81; explains Spanish policy toward Will-

ing, 81–82; orders Willing to return British property, 82–83; negotiations with Captain Nunn, 89–90; orders return of *Speedwell*, 92; pressures Willing to leave Louisiana, 95–96; assists Americans in returning to Illinois, 98; employs agents in Pensacola and Mobile, 101–102; response to British activity along the Mississippi, 110–112; campaign against Manchac and Baton Rouge, 112–115; 119–122; orders occupation of Natchez, 123–125; assessment of his Mississippi campaign, 126; leads assault on Mobile, 126–130; lays siege to Pensacola, 131–133; policy toward Natchez, 133–134; reaction to Natchez rebellion, 139–140; treatment of Natchez rebels, 142–143; pardons Natchez rebels, 150–151.
Gálvez, José de, Minister of the Indies, 36.
George III, reaction to Willing's Raid, 105.
George, Robert, Captain, 63, 98.
Germain, Lord George, 39, 40, 60, 105, 108, 109, 115.
German Mercenaries, 105–106, 114, 131. *See also* Waldeck.
Gibson, George, Captain: leads expedition down the Mississippi, 33–34; activities of in New Orleans, 34–36; departure from New Orleans, 40, 51.
Graham, John J., Lieutenant, 117, 119.
Graiden, Alexander, 31, 91–92.
Grand-Pré, Carlos de, 122–123, 142, 144.
Great Britain: policy toward West Florida, 4–7; relations with Choctaw Indians, 10; failure to protect western settlements, 11; Spanish policy toward, 49; fear of Spanish